Dr. J. L. Carter

DARE
TO
LIVE

Understanding Terminal Illness

"When the Grasshopper Becomes a Burden"

— Ecclesiastes :d

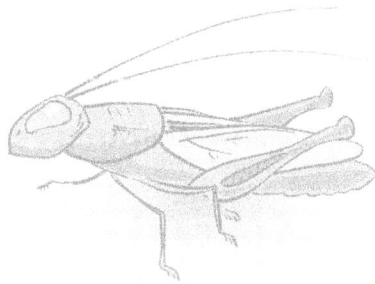

All Biblical quotations are from the NJAVE Version unless otherwise noted.

TANK Publishing
Baltimore, MD

Design:
Concepts Unlimited
wow.Conceptualization.coma

ISBN-13: 978-0-69222-572-1   (pbk)
ISBN-10: 0692225722

14   15   16   17   18
0 9 8 7 6 5 4 3 2 1

First Printing, 2014
Printed in the United States of America

ACKNOWLEDGEMENTS

*T*he Word of God tells us, "in everything to give thanks." I want to thank God, with a sincere heart, for allowing me to complete this task that was started a very long time ago. I thank God for the energy that was needed. I thank God for the persons who encouraged me continuously to stay the course.

I want to thank Annie Chiles for her constant support and help in making sure I did not take the easy way out, but remained faithful to the assignment. Sister Annie, you are forever in my prayers.

I wish to thank my dear friends, many who are preachers, for their gentle push and encouragement not to abort the assignment.

To the people I serve and love with an unconditional love, I wish to thank Ark Church. I will always give thanks for the bond that exist between Pastor and congregation. Your love and support towards me as your Pastor has been immeasurable. Your confidence in me is most humbling and was a rich deposit into this work. My life has expanded positively and my growth in the Lord has increased tremendously because of you.

I want to thank my family for all the love and support extended to me during this time of writing. Particularly, I thank God for a wonderful daughter, Kellie

James, who made certain that my stress level stayed at a minimum doing during my writing time. She knew what needed to be done and freed up my calendar which enhanced my desire to complete this work.

I thank God for a wife who gives a greater meaning to the words "helpmeet" and "soul companion." My wife, Cora is truly connected to me in every way imaginable and more. She has experienced my emotional roller coaster when doing something of this magnitude. Her patience, her flowing with my unpredictable demeanor and her impeccable and flawless love for me is more than I deserve. I am so glad, enormously glad, God chose me to be the soul recipient of her love. *I love my wife and I love my life.*

Again, I want to thank everyone who laid hands on this work, seen and unseen, that it might bless those who find themselves living with a terminal illness or being the caretaker of a terminally patient.

TABLE OF CONTENTS

We only have
one life to live,
therefore we should
live life to the fullest.

PROLOGUE

$\mathcal{L}$ ife is precious and we only have one life to live, therefore one should live life to the fullest. Each day that one is afforded another God given privilege, one should to take advantage of every opportunity that crosses one's path in life and that person should be thankful. To be able to walk through open doors and embrace new experiences that are presented daily is immeasurable. To move through life knowing that this is not a dress rehearsal but the real deal allows every day to be a good day.

The criteria to determine the worth or the wealth of a person is often measured in hard currency, financial portfolios and in celebrated and legendary relationships. Such realities cannot be ignored and should be recognized for what they are. One might suggest having a genuine, loving and caring family is a higher measure of wealth and to share blessings with others is experiencing life on a grand scale. To experience babies evolving from a newborn to childhood, to adolescence and to adulthood and carving out a healthy productive niche for themselves in today's world is most invigorating. The joy of finding your soul mate is an indescribable joy.

Wealth, joy and happiness have a higher standard that excels beyond the tangible but is anchored in those intangibles that is sometimes taken for granted.

Death is the common dominator that we all must face. Death does not discriminate among black and white, rich and poor, Hispanic, Asian or religious affiliations. Death is a reality that brings about a permanent change that is always difficult to accommodate. Academically speaking, we know death is coming; we are sometimes given certain signs and warning that death is near but one can never adequately prepare for an experience that can overwhelm and cause great pain to the strongest of humanity and family members.

Terminal illness becomes the path that leads to death. When a person has been diagnosed with an aggressive and inoperable form of cancer, life for the patient and the patient's family changes drastically. Everything that existed before the diagnosis is no longer in place. The joy, the laughter, the play, light hearted jokes and the excitement for life have been evicted from the mindset of the patient and the patient's family and the environment seems permanently melancholy. Yet, for the terminally ill and the family of the terminally ill, life does not have to be over. In the midst of an unfavorable diagnosis, the terminally ill patient has some control over the outcome of the matter and the period of transitioning.

As God said to Adam and Eve, "the day that you eat of this tree you will surely die." Once we are born, we are placed on the road that may one day lead to terminal illness. We cannot avoid death, but we can navigate our steps that lead to death. Persons who are faced with terminal illness and their family members are often without information and help when experiencing the hard realities of this life-threatening illness. Once the reality of death has been embraced, it is my belief and understanding that eternal freedom can be experienced and one is no longer caught in a context of the constant fear of death. Jesus himself, the Son of God, but very human, makes the statement, "no one takes my life but I lay it down." The terminally ill person is the one who decides his/her last breath. She or he is the one who declares when it's over and until that time life is to be experienced and managed with human dignity.

My hope and prayer for persons who are terminally ill and who have been told by medical professional to put their house in order is that they would discover the inner strength to stand tall in knowing that their last days can be free of fear of the unknown and constant worry. One's last days can be great days with family and friends.

Touch is life
extending itself to life.
It is the fellowship
and infusion of caring.

SECTION I: ARRIVING AT THE TERMINAL

Chapter 1

THE UNEXPECTED TRIP
TO THE TERMINAL

*T*here is a rocking chair motionless, sitting in the corner of a room. A basketball is trapped behind the water heater in the garage. The children's swing is tied in silence, hanging motionless. Tools are gathering dust in an unused and darkened shed. In the once busy kitchen, lights are turned off and nothing is simmering on the stove. Is it mother, father, sister, brother, child or friend who is here and yet not here? Who is missing from the moment? Here in this place emptiness is filling the mind of one who still lives. The vacant signs are throughout the household. There is an indication of change disturbing the stability and usualness of life. Fear and dread have invaded the brave hearted and there is a breach that cannot be repaired.

Life can be as uncertain as driving in the fog, trusting the lights of the car in front of you because you can't see your way. You are proceeding slowly, anxiously, in uncertainty, fighting to maintain control and confidence, in a growing darkness. Hope diminishes as you await the miracle burst of light to shatter the darkness. The fog seems without end, going on as it blankets everything. Yesterday's surety is now hidden; it has become obscured by the fog of a dismal tomorrow. Hidden behind every turn you make are, for certain, dangers. This is overwhelming. This is a simple visualization of the necessity of "Presence" needed for the terminally ill.

As a pastor for over twenty seven years, I am convinced that ministry must be a deliberate preparation and reparation. We repair and build up broken, wasted and abandoned places. We give structure and aid in the preparation for new walkways in the lives of the people. We help them to hold on to life and we prepare them to let go of life on this earth. We speak light into the *darkness and life* and into dead and dying situations. We breathe hope to the despairing and eternity in the midst of our temporal humanity. Ministry is not reactionary; it is provisional foresight which meets life needs that will surely come. It should not manifest in an emergency, but is preparatory, waiting to activate as situations arise. It has a readiness prepared to meet the need. Ministry is a deliberate and foreseeing plan of action.

Life once lived in simplicity can suddenly be filled with confusion, frustration and anguish as we wish for the former days. As children, we played in the fields of endless time and we listened to the words of our elders, not understanding the weight or worth of them. They were words of wisdom which became trusted friends, helping us to cross the busy streets of life and arrive safely on the other side. One phrase that I so vividly remember is, *"the candle glows its brightest just before it goes out."* I have sat in the flickering flame of a candle's end and experienced its brilliance. It's one clear flash, in addition to a burst of light, overcoming the darkness, which initiates and finalizes with certainty, the end.

I have seen the light of a cozy romantic dinner, when the electricity was out. And I have seen the light at the bedside of a passing loved one.

The last days of our lives, no matter how long or short, express the essence of what, who and whose we are. It is not the weariness of the flesh, but the hope and expectancy of life that lasts forever. It is a hard and determined task not to allow the life fire to extinguish prematurely. However all things are not in our hands as our days are appointed. Yet, just as a workman breaks open a smoldering log to release the fire held within it, our "presence" helps the fire of life to break out during the last minutes of life, helping the terminally ill release their light into the life beyond.

Terminal illness is a common phrase used in and outside the medical arena. Simply put, terminal illness is the phrase used when facing imminent death because of disease or sickness. When the doctor brings back a prognosis that is hopeless and that seemingly points to death, the caregiver or a devoted loved one is faced with the great challenge of providing supportive care, encouragement and inspiration to the person who is terminally ill. At that point, a genuine bond with the person experiencing terminal illness must be fostered. Knowing or believing that life is running out, both patient and caregiver begin counting the days.

When ministering to the terminally ill, it is imperative and vitally important that we are aware of the resources available in this area. As ministers, counselors, caregivers, medical professionals, family members and friends, we must demonstrate a ministry of "presence" in the present life of the terminally ill. We must be mindful of the fact that not only is our physical presence important, but that the terminally ill person is still present in this life as well. This thoughtful consideration is a foundation and the anchor of certainty in an uncertain time. It gives the terminally ill the assurance that someone cares and is with them as they chart a course through uncertain and troubled waters. Presence is the help and the hope one needs while traveling through the difficult days ahead.

To effectively develop a ministry for the terminally ill, we must develop a healthy approach in our understanding of terminal illness and become familiar with both the scientific/medical and traditional biblical views of sickness. The information in the Old and New Testaments is a marriage laced with the understanding of Jesus' presence. Throughout the Bible, one can see many examples of healing being associated with the preached word of Jesus.

There is a direct correlation between teaching and healing. In one Bible passage, Jesus was said to have had healing in the borders of his garment. Mark 2:17 reports the Savior saying, *"They who are well need not a physician, those who are whole need no physician. I have come for those who are sick, not whole: those who are in need of healing."* Terminal illness and readiness to minister to those with terminal illness also existed in biblical times. People were in need of hope, healing, support, encouragement and salvation. Jesus came with everything necessary in His embodiment. Even today, Jesus comes for those in need.

To the terminally ill, preaching is inspirational, comforting, converting and preparatory. It provides companionship and hope in the journey, reminding the terminally ill that they are not alone. The foundation for our premise and understanding is that *"Preaching is healing for the terminally ill."* Persons who are terminally ill, whether in a coma or not, whether mobile or immobile, can still hear. The listening ear is the receiver of the gospel which is good news.

Did you know the last sense to leave the body at the time of death is hearing? This fact substantiated by medical documentation is miraculous. Therefore, for the terminally ill patient who is presented with the gospel, healing is possible. Regardless of the medical prognosis, we live and walk by faith. We dare to encourage others by faith amidst impossibility; God is able to do the impossible. *(Luke 1:37)* The good news of the gospel is the ignition, the starter for faith and healing. Patients can respond, negatively or positively, because hearing is operational. Utilizing what I refer to as the three P's of "Presence," great comfort and tremendous support are provided to those with terminal illness. The three P's are **persistence**, **presentation** and **preparation**.

To utilize the (3P's) of "Presence" we stay actively involved in the condition of the terminally ill. Persistence continues is in spite of changes or shifting attitudes, medical condition, hopelessness or weariness for the patient. We humbly and consistently help in spite of the daily transitions or circumstances. Our presentation is thoughtful and individualized as we apply truth, infused with hope, considering the condition and concerns of the patient. Our preparation is an in touch acknowledgment of the changing condition of the patient. We must maintain a careful and prayerful readiness for the daily rigors of emotions that are due to change or lack of change. It is keeping informed of the progression of the condition, which enables us to encourage and inspire the patient and their family members. As we remain in communion with God through prayer, we are effective and relevant in the ministry of hope and the "Presence" we provide.

The big business of life, like many other corporate businesses, has many supporting departments contributing to its overall condition, effectiveness and causes. For smooth operations, all supporting departments should operate corporately to insure the stability of the firm. When one department has an operational failure or its performance level drops, it affects the overall function of the company. It can cause a shut down or ruin the entire operation. The other departments must increase productivity to handle the additional strain of a non productive area. When operational shutdowns are being experienced throughout the entire corporation, the firm will suffer a lack of productivity, revenues will decrease and in most probability, the firm will be forced to shut down.

Terminal illnesses are the shutdown of the support systems sustaining life. We live in a world of fast breaking advancements in education, computer technology, publications, iPods, iPads, iPhones with immediate global access via the internet and a multiplicity of communication devices. We can be in continual communication as we text, Facebook and tweet. We experience medical breakthrough on a daily basis. Organ and facial transplants, enhancements and wonder drugs like cyclosporine and azidothymidline [AZT] give us great hope for the future. With daily advancements we could almost convince ourselves that we are superheroes, invincible and out of the reach of the final effects of anything, until the medical prognosis of terminal illness occurs.

The ability to successfully treat many diseases such as tuberculosis, malaria, small pox and other illnesses should translate into a healthier existence. However more viruses are finding their way into mainstream life. Sometimes it has been the cure weakening the body and making it susceptible to new viruses and diseases which have become resistant to the advanced treatments as quickly as they are discovered. We are continually faced with new incurable viruses. They are life threatening and terminating illnesses. A terminal diagnosis means medical professionals consider the disease hopeless. These diseases include cancer, AIDS, Alzheimer's, end stage kidney failure, lupus and more.

There are many definitions and terminologies associated with terminal illness. Physicians do not necessarily agree with the preacher or biblical interpretation when referring to terminal illness. Many patients will not agree with the doctor or the preacher in their definition of terminal illness. This miscommunication adds more frustration, confusion and hopelessness than either party intended. Words are important and the choice of words can make all the difference in how and what happens once they are spoken. Words should be chosen carefully to be effective, both physiologically and spiritually, because words and personal definitions affect people and their responses.

The word "terminal" is perplexing for many because it is used loosely. When we use the term terminal in relationship to an illness the same word applies to infants, adolescents, adults and seniors; all are struggling to maintain the life that is in them. They are in a life battle, while their bodies are experiencing shutdown. This picture alone adds a new dimension to the ministry and service we provide as a supportive spiritual respirator. We help one to breathe in a breathless situation.

Death is an alien and a hostile intruder invading the life of the patient. What does this mean for the patient who has been given what is apparently a death sentence without hope for reprieve? How does one internalize a concept which is alien to the spirit? How fixed, how permanent and how concrete are the words that have diagnosed a patient to be terminally ill? Does this mean the person who has tested positive for HIV should lie down, die today and forget tomorrow? Does it mean the cancer patient should stop all treatment because death is inevitable? Does it also mean all hopes and aspirations for healing both physically and spiritually are forever lost in some eternal vacuum or suspended in oblivion? What are the limits? What are the boundaries? What is the definition one gives to terminal illness? Is it some type of permanent red light stopping the traffic of our existence?

Medically defined, a terminal illness is one that ends with the death of the patient. There is no cure, no antidote and no remedy; there is only treatment. Often a person can be in a vegetative state or an irreversible coma, unable to communicate with family and loved ones. They are unable to communicate pain, fear, hope or desires. In many ways they have become nonfunctional, part of the invisible visible and often void of the sensitivity and warmth coming from one hand touching another. In this state of unconsciousness, touch care is vital. Each touch demonstrates connection, strength, inclusion, help and the assurance of not being alone. Touch assures the patient they are still being considered and included; they have not been abandoned. ***Touch is life extending itself to life. It is the fellowship and infusion of caring.***

Conditions are considered terminal when the following exists:
- Prescribed medicines are no longer effective
- The patient's state of health is deteriorating
- The body no longer fights to overcome the illness
- The illness continues to overwhelm the patient, beating the body into subjection

The final stage of the terminal illness is often an irreversible comatose state. The body is being overwhelmed, overcome and stops its heroic fight. When all the above conditions are apparent, a sense of defeat is in the atmosphere. It hovers in the room and all who enter are able to sense hopelessness and resignation. At this stage the medical condition has declined and recovery or intervention is improbable. Medical professionals have used up their resources and only comfort and basic life maintenance is being done. The cold reality of all the medical data collected, the test results and the medical teams are in agreement with the terminal prognosis. Medical intervention ceases and the reality of impending death is apparent as experts have exhausted their options.

Our world is filled with known and unknown experts. We have at our fingertips access to the work and study of the world. In the process of this writing I have interviewed technicians, medical practitioners and professionals for a genuine understanding in the area of terminal illness. I have listened to personal reflections of patients, physicians, physiologists, family members, hospice workers and observers of every type. As a pastor, I have countless hours of "Presence" experience. For certain, man will come to the end of his capability and his knowledge. When limits are exceeded and we have exhausted our knowledge, we begin speaking of the inevitability. However, in my understanding, the inevitability is life now and eternally. It is life that ends in this world but does not end and is full of victory and expectation.

As we consider what the patient has lost, we must also consider what they currently value. Any good accountant will not only measure losses but also assets and gains. Yes, there are limits and obstacles but there are also inclusions and hope. When all other senses are gone, even the sensation or ability to respond to touch or move a muscle, the patient can still hear everything going on in their environment. It can be called *the song in the night season of life* or *the infusion of faith.* When things may appear to be empty and failing in the terminally ill, hearing is operational. Even when the patient's life is supported by respirators and their eyelids close, patients can still hear. In a later chapter, I will discuss this last sense to remain, the hearing or the auditory life line.

"Presence" can also include speaking. We must remain mindful of what will be heard in words and in our tone. We take the necessary time to refresh ourselves so our tiredness is not interpreted as weariness or defeat. We consider carefully and prayerfully what to say and what not to say. Our words must be meaningful and not the idle chatter of religious aspirations. We are experiencing the rigors of the illness with the terminally ill and are touched by the feelings of their infirmity. Our hearts are not calloused; we also want the miracle of life for and in them. We want to see faith overcoming the power of the disease challenging their life. We want to see them walking away, carrying their bed of affliction, evidencing victory. We carry in ourselves the knowledge that death is swallowed up in victory and we want desperately to experience the victory with them. Our words must be seasoned with the salt of wisdom, patience, purpose and faith.

There are no greater words than God's word. Our words and His word together provide help and hope in our daily conversations to the patient. Remember, we are God's agents of hope and the power of His presence. We are the watering pot and He is the one giving increase. He is there in us and through us, providing hope and love to the dying. He is so concerned about their life struggle that He called us along side to give the patient His word of His truth and life. What we say matters and how we say it matters. We are called to share, *"Lo I am with **you** always"* as effectively and powerfully as we share *"Arise and walk,"* because Jesus said both statements. We have been given the privilege and responsibility to speak into the last months, days or hours of their lives the words they will take with them forever.

The terminally ill will experience varying attitudes about God in this process of illness. We must represent His presence accurately. We cannot be defensive, but we must be patient and deliberate in our responses. I cannot overemphasize the deliberateness of what we are called to do. We must be prepared and ready to be effective. We exercise the power of silence and listening. Terminally ill patients may need to express their concerns and even their fears. Not every comment needs to be examined and not every action of God needs to be justified. Sometimes the terminally ill person and their families need freedom to express their frustration and fears openly. We can evaluate what is reactionary and what is truth. Death is an unexpected hostile takeover; "Presence" is being there for the announcement, process and conclusion of the matter as we bring assurance that God has the final word in the situation.

It is not enough for the terminally ill to hear us, we must also hear them to effectively address their concerns with a genuine measure of satisfaction. We have no prepared script, but we are challenged to provide genuine support. They need time and opportunity to vent their frustrations. These frustrations, fears, angers, confusions and disappointments, if not vocalized, add to their deteriorating medical condition. By practicing our own hearing we open the door for self expression when possible. We usher in the peace that ends the internal battle of faith. For the comatose patient we can anticipate and verbalize for them some possible areas of anxieties while ushering in and providing the comfort of "Presence" and faith. In this way we apply medicine for the healing to the soul even when the body is failing.

The power of hearing is important to both the terminally ill and to those who care for them during this time. It is important to the family to not just be bombarded with our words but to know we hear their concerns. Hearing is important to the caretakers who daily attend to the terminally ill and may not see any results for their labor. We help them to understand, manage and translate their frustration in a healthy, productive manner to prevent feelings of guilt. We keep on hearing until the very last moments; we listen intently for changes in their speech and the breathing of the patient. We cannot fill an already full space. By hearing, we make room for the terminally ill to discharge negatives and receive the power of the *Words of Eternal Life.* As we listen, we hear and respond to the doors left open to usher in His presence.

What we say and how we say it matters as it inspires. To inspire is to breathe into and to stimulate energy, ideas and reverence for God. As we inspire, we arouse the hope that is already in the terminally ill in spite of the facts and evidence of the illness. Terminally ill people do not want to die; they want to live in spite of the diagnosis they have received. We come bearing life in the word we speak and the ministry we provide. We come to care for those who are dying that they may, in the last hours, embrace life fully and live forever in His fullness.

We come to confirm that life is still an option for the terminally ill. Even in the state they are in they have the power to choose life. Without a listening ear, how can we know when the door is open and the individual is ready to transition to the newness of eternal life.

Sensitivity on the part
of the caregiver
allows the patient to breathe
between sips of reality.

Chapter 2

THE ONRAMP TO THE TERMINAL

*T*o be effective one must first be intentional and deliberate when relating to the terminally ill. God utilizes many voices to speak to us. We are often so busy in our everyday responsibilities that we are oblivious of a *God moment.* He may speak in obvious ways and other times by the subtlety of a little whisper, a fragrance or a still cameo moment. Regardless of how He makes His intention known, it is powerful and purposeful. Keeping ourselves prayerful allows us to be sensitive to His voice and His speaking even in the ordinariness of life. I cannot stress enough the value and worth of prayer, not only as we speak to God but as a listening tool so we don't miss the important appointments for purpose in our lives. Those quiet times of prayer and those listening moments with Him equip and intensify our ability to hear what the patient is actually saying and not just the words they say.

One day I was riding in my neighborhood, not being the pastor, just a neighbor. I had gone into a local store and was pulling out of a parking space. Just then I noticed a sign in the window of the car behind me. It caught my eye; it was a for sale sign. My wife and I had been looking for a gas efficient car for everyday travel and this seemed to be just what we needed. The owner of the car had deliberately put the sign in the window to catch the eye of potential buyers like myself. Her plan had worked. I gave the car a "once over" look and considered if this car would answer our personal needs. It was then I felt that gentle nudge, the push I have become all too familiar with. It was the whisper into my inner hearing, encouraging my expectation of God.

The woman selling the car was bright and friendly in her mannerism. As I approached the car she quickly announced what a great car it was. She had no complaints about the car and hated to part with it. I wondered why she wanted to sell it if it was such a great car. She looked intently at me as if anticipating my response. Then she simply informed me she had been diagnosed with a terminal illness. In living out the last days of her life, she desired to make things easier for her husband who would be left to handle everything. She knew he wasn't going to need this car and so she planned to sell it so he won't have to. It would be one less thing he would have to do. "Presence" was already in my spirit and her presence and active participation in light of the diagnosis of terminal illness was a whisper of confirmation for me to "hear."

Often like Elijah, we stand at the top of the mountain awaiting some great sign from God concerning the course of our lives. We want to see miracles and hear the sounds of His motion on our behalf. He may choose to speak to us and our purpose in the stillest and smallest of voices. The whisper of purpose is powerful, whether it comes from a large marching band or the sound of gentle rain. When God speaks, it is life changing. His sheep should be listening and attentive to His speaking. These words give actualization to purpose, acknowledgement, confirmation and direction to us. God is revealing and commissioning us to go forward and do our assignment. "Presence" was already in its infancy in me and now God was confirming and encouraging me to move even further in that direction. What a powerful advertisement of life! This woman was actively taking charge of what was diagnosed as *her last days*.

Here was this woman who had in her possession something for me. She didn't know what it was, but I was listening. She may have thought it was the car, which at first, caught my eye. Yet, it was more than the car; it was her determination to be a part of the life process as long as possible. She had my undivided attention for those moments. What I received from her will last a lifetime. She was responding to her diagnosis of terminal illness by taking control and being a part of the process. I listened to her sales pitch but what I heard was, "I am taking control of my life while I can; after all it is my life." She was demonstrating a determination to live and love her family for as long as she could. She talked freely of her illness as she bargained about the car; after all it was a part of her life and it was already becoming a part of mine. She was as deliberate in her take-charge attitude, as I was in mine to grasp the concept of "Presence."

Many terminally ill patients respond differently to their diagnoses. Some are passive, some depressive and some are aggressive. They act out what they feel and their feelings may change from day to day. As supporters, caretakers, family members and medical professionals, we should expect all these responses. They cannot be categorized as good or bad, but simply, responses to physical and spiritual invasion. It is an extreme crisis of the body as it systematically begins to shut down. The mind is trying to maintain control of an *out of control* situation. The spirit is fighting fear with faith and ignoring the facts, will not change the predicted outcome. Clicking our little red shoes and wishing we were in Kansas will not prevent the storm. We struggle to understand how in one moment faith can move mountains and in the next it has to accept the limits of reality.

Many people develop and display denial and isolation as a coping mechanism when faced with devastating news and become disillusioned. It is "the just leave me alone" or "this isn't happening to me" response. The ability to think or reason amidst this crisis can be illogical, disconnected and inconsistent. There is an inner hysteria which must be released in one form or another. It can be heard in statements which reject facts. When people reject reality, they also reject any possibility of solutions or fullness. We may hear statements such as, "This is not happening to me. They got my test mixed up with someone else's. I am too young to face death." And of course patients may ask, "Why is God allowing this to happen to me?" These statements are normal and understandable responses. They are common and require sensitive listening, open understanding, sincere prayer and care. Denial is refusing to accept a natural truth. It does not display faith at work. Faith allows us to accept a natural truth while trusting in a greater spiritual truth. Faith can intensify as it meets resistance or unreasonableness. Faith can defy logic and overcome fear.

These responses function as a buffer after the unexpected and shocking news. The news without expression doesn't evidence acceptance of the fact and can nullify our faith. We may know something, yet knowing it doesn't mean we receive it with all its personal baggage. The fact must impact us as a reality so faith can go to work. It is like going to the airport and picking up the passenger and leaving the luggage. We are expecting our miracle amidst the finality on the part of medical professionals. Faith is not built into the medical practitioner's equation. Their finality isn't something we prepare ourselves for. The initial responses of the patient do not mean at some later time the same person will not be willing, ready or even welcome to talk about what is coming. It may not be embraced but can be dealt with on their terms. It is when the patient is ready and at their convenience that we are able to share constructive, nourishing, comforting and reinforcing words to help the patient, not the listener, face the issue at hand. We speak measured and flexible words into the hearing of the patient to strengthen and prepare them for the inevitable. We actively listen intently to know what, when and how to respond.

It is impossible to pour more water in an already filled glass without spillage and clean up. As helpers we are observant to sense the volume capacity of the patient. When the patient is already full with more than they can hold, we don't carelessly continue to pour into their full vessel. This is a good rule of thumb; don't pour in more than the patient is able to receive at any given time. Your words should be measured to the current capacity. Being sensitive to the patient means you are ready to start or stop as they have need. **Sensitivity on the part of the caregiver allows the patient to breathe between sips of reality.** By exercising perceptive listening and hearing disciplines, we leave the door open to revisit important conversation areas at later dates. We don't want to push our way into conversations, talking about death when the patient is at their lowest time or when they need a listening ear and not a talking mouth.

We have become accustomed to preventive care in our society. Preventive care can include talking in advance of an actual terminal illness diagnosis. These talks are tools helping to seed and store faith, to precede the facts. They can provide a healthier, stronger ability and a better perception. The patient can revisit a conversation they have already had without having to start from the initial onset. We don't have to continue hitting the nail of impending death to effectively converse about terminal illness. These advance conversations will give us a better concept of the patient's thoughts and desires. This will help in the event the patient is unable to voice their wishes later. It is beneficial to have informative family conversations during a healthy time instead of a fragile time. These talks provide information about the arrangements for both the financial and spiritual security of the patient, family and others involved in their lives. They are less stressful when the household is still functioning with a regular and reliable income and without the addition of medical expenses due to the current terminal illness diagnosis.

When we postpone or delay these talks, it is not in the best interest of the patient or the family. Our failure to have these advanced talks often evidences our own defensiveness and denial. Like children, we believe if we close our eyes or don't talk about a thing, it will not happen; postponement is a liability and not an asset. Death is not a friend; it is an enemy. Discussing strategies before one becomes weak and feeble gives the patient the opportunity to take the aggressive stand. It will also help the family not to feel the pressure or guilt of making decisions of uncertainty. These *pre-event* talks help the patient and family to bond while making the very important decisions of living life to its fullest.

Denial should be a temporary defense, which will be replaced by partial acceptance. We are moving into measurable areas of confronting truth. The patient's partial acceptance is not an overnight process or something that can be expected or experienced immediately. It is often the opposite, especially when the patient learns that their days are numbered and given a countdown of the time remaining. When absolutes are spoken such as, there isn't a current cure available, or when the patient hears medicine has reached the extent of its abilities, man is now putting a number to the days that are left; at this point denial is normal. Partial acceptance varies from person to person and can change from day to day. It is not uncommon for persons to appear to accept today and reject tomorrow. Prayer, persistence and patience continue to encourage the patient; they are not left to fight this battle alone.

Denial, for some, becomes the avenue by which they are able to cope with their terminal illness, a fact that cannot be avoided. The medical prognosis can't be pushed aside and the terminal illness is a reality. Somewhere in the recesses of the patient's mind these facts concerning their illness are very real. After all, they have evidence of the illness in their own bodies. Denial allows the patient a way to acknowledge the facts, yet, move in a direction that suggests, "I am still going on with my life." The patient, like the woman selling her car, is in a courageous battle. Rather than focusing on the morbidity and negative reality of the terminal diagnosis, one forges ahead with his or her life. They begin focusing on the same things that once brought joy to the heart, like trading in the car and pressing for the best price. They focus on getting a win in the midst of what others may see as a great loss. The patient begins to live beyond or above their personal plight of terminal illness and, although they know they are facing imminent death, they make a positive decision to make the best of the time left. It is hands on and taking control which is a place of power in the midst of the illness that manifests daily.

Denial can come in the form of denying any changes in appearance because of weight loss/gain, hair loss, loss of energy levels or skin changes. It may include making jokes to deal with the physical changes. It may include going on a shopping spree to buy new clothes with a splash of color to compensate for the altered physique. Making the best of the last days is doing whatever it takes to face death with a positive and victorious acknowledgment that all is yet well. Death is not the end; this is the place where faith meets the natural limits of truth. We help the patient to celebrate daily victories while embracing life. Denial, which at first seems unreasonable as non-acceptance, is now being replaced by the day to day battle strategy for life and joy, even in the midst of a terminal illness.

Every day life in a crisis presents a new opportunity for a win in what would appear to be a losing situation. It is the daily victory of overcoming the inevitable. The patient is fighting back and taking control of their lives again. One may say, "This may be happening to me, but the fact is, I will fight it with every ounce of my being and live each day fully until I live again."

We have to learn to wear the pink and purple ribbons for those who are engaged in the warfare of life regardless of the diagnosis. We are the support team that rallies around the home team, cheering every accomplishment and helping them on the days when fatigue overwhelms them. We give them the space to complain and to be angry without trying to always redirect them. We can even join them in their anger when needed because every day is a very important day for them and us. It is a day that the Lord has made and despite the current conditions, we will push to rejoice and be glad in it. Every day is a new day of beginnings and there is sufficient joy to be found in everyday with hope.

Isolation is another part of denial. Barriers are often erected in life to avoid contact with reality. These barriers prevent truth from being realized. These barriers are erected to stand between the patient and reality, between the hopelessness and the help available and often act as a shield to protect. The patient is shut in and cut off, no longer interested in the world, which includes family and friends. There is no interest in the daily activity of a world they still live in. The patient doesn't want to participate in life. Viewing television, neither listening to the radio nor having conversations is no longer of interest. They are punishing themselves and their desire to live and the future diminishes daily. The patient may even communicate they just want to be left alone. Being left alone with their fears and anger is a place of torment.

Isolation can cause rejection of the fellowship and love of family and friends who want to spend time with them. The patient seeks to isolate himself from the activity of yesterday when everything was normal and live in defeat in a non-functional existence. This can be seen as counting the days and resigning from life. They live as a recluse, refusing to fulfill the days they have. We must present "Presence." Even when not wanted to do so, we still must remain patiently and lovingly persistent. The quiet intrusion into the shell they have encased themselves in requires skill. Like a hatchling, we must use our special beak or ability to persistently tap away at the isolation, breaking through without being intrusive or abusive. The knowledge that prayer and patience prevails, helps during these shut out times. Care giving is available to help and not hurt the patient who is very much still the living. Even for those who are comatose we continue to be active in their hearing. We do not allow them to shut down but to experience the peace and assurance of "Presence" in their present life.

The walls of isolation should not be demolished with a sledge hammer but with the gentle pulling and prodding of compassion. We listen and watch for the smallest entry place and we understand that the patient has a lot to adjust to and we help as much as we can. "Presence" cannot be accomplished if we are absent, offended, uncertain or whining. Like the *Energizer Bunny*, we continue beating the drum and going forward with the knowledge that isolation isn't locking us out but it is trapping the patient in. This reaction can also suffocate the life out of the patient and drain them of hope. Although we are patient, we are consistently tugging at the walls being built. We evidence their importance by our refusal to be left out of their lives and we validate their current life.

We cannot attempt to bring
our sense of order
to the disorder and chaos
of terminal illness.
We can help in understanding
the validity of the anger and
not allow it to discourage us
from continuing to be available
and helpful.

Chapter 3

THE BUSYNESS OF THE TERMINAL

*H*ave you ever broken down on the side of the road with hot steam billowing and mixing in the blue skies just above your car? Your eyes are darting back and forth, watching for any sign of roadside assistance. Not only is your car overheating, but so are you because the needed help hasn't arrived. The steam from your radiator mixing with the hot summer air keeps your temperature rising and you are boiling. Have you ever noticed this usually happens on the day when you have the most appointments? Have you ever felt like the rabbit in "Alice in Wonderland" being late for a very important date? At this point you feel helpless and there isn't anything to do but wait on the help you are not sure will come. You are fuming and constantly looking at your watch as if either action will change today's events. Why today, why when you were so close to your destination and when you have so many other plans? You regularly have your car maintenance done and the engine serviced. You haven't been careless with your car like some people you know. You pay for the roadside assistance with your insurance and you have never used it. So now when you need them they are delayed. They are off helping someone else in the middle of your crisis. You are experiencing frustration, anger and the feeling of help-lessness during a breakdown.

We don't always understand and equate grief with the terminally ill, as we do hopelessness. They are the sup-porting cast of the anger that is now brewing, boiling and spewing out from within the patient. We want the terminally ill to understand that as long as there is life there is hope and at the same time we want them to get their affairs in order. The duplicity of the message is the place where the fresh and salt waters are trying to mix and the patient is only seeing the impossibility of the mixture. You are asking them to hope and halt at the same time. You want them to run and stand still, as if they will gain ground in this action. It will seem point-less to keep playing the game if you cannot win or if the other team has all the advantages and even the coaches on their side. When the press releases the play-by-play coverage, revealing the other team is winning by a land-slide, why continue playing the last minutes of the game?

Anger is a human emotion that often leaves a person feeling negative. It simply makes a bad situation worse, but it is a normal reaction. We all have experienced it, even while help is on the way. It is that silent scream that can't find its way without saying, "why me" and "why now." It is the loss of control we experience when we have to depend on someone else's intervention. It is not having a definitive solution in sight. It is when our options are limited or nonexistent. You are angry because this should not be happening especially when you took all the necessary precautions and followed the *manufacturer's suggested maintenance.* You are now stuck in the middle of your day, in the middle of your life. You are stuck in traffic and your plans are uncertain. This is not the outcome you had in mind when the day began. Some may say it is just frustration but we all know it is anger. You have spent the entire day putting the puzzle together, just to get to the end and find important pieces missing.

There are often two specific types of anger. One is anger that can be understood or explained. The source of this anger can be revealed and possibly reconciled with logic. The questions can be almost satisfied with basic logic or realities. We can help the patient reason through this type of anger. It is manageable, controllable and although the patient doesn't like the procedure or the situation, the reasoning is based on life's logic. This anger can also propel the patient into a reasonable resistance that can provide a level of success or ease the current distress. The treatment is curative and essential, bringing a positive result; it is defendable as being necessary.

The other anger cannot be understood or explained,

it is those *why questions* which have no answers. This is a destructive volatile anger affecting the patient's overall condition. The patient is working a relentless Rubik's cube and no matter how they turn it, the colors do not line up and fall into place. The frustration continues to build and before you know it the anger is all consuming. The patient is affecting everyone in their sphere of influence and everyone who cares about them experiences their rage. This anger is often accompanied by feelings of futility which spawn rage, and is counterproductive to the patient's condition. The anger does not allow or afford the patient any momentary successes or relief. It is relentless and begins to gather to itself every action or inaction around it to fuel unpleasant and negative thoughts. This anger doesn't have any gain incorporated in it and is therefore utterly destructive and defeating to the patient.

Take for example the mother of seven and faithful church worker who is devoted to her husband and family. She has served on the usher ministry, never smoked a cigarette and has now been diagnosed with breast and lung cancer. After motherhood, marriage, 44 years of life, cancer now is in both breasts and the lungs. She followed good medical practices by having annual and even semiannual checkups. She incorporated positive dietary habits and exercise into her life and still she is terminally ill. When first diagnosed, she followed every instruction and was the model patient of endurance as she put up a courageous fight. She went to the support group where she heard the testimonies of those who endured the wretchedness of the illness, but have recovered. Now her life choices appear to be pointless and unrewarding in the face of her terminal diagnosis.

This disappointment and frustration hurts and it angers the patient. It is the stimulus that promotes anger which cannot be fully explained by reason. There is no legitimate source to answer the *why or how* questions the patient often asks. The mother is made bitter because of the lack of a hopeful prognosis. It would be easier to explain a situation like this if the mother had smoked four packs of cigarettes daily. It would still hurt, but the why questions could be satisfied. The anger with unanswered questions is very real and very disturbing to the terminally ill patient and their families. These questions are unanswered because in reality there are no answers to the "why me" question.

The terminally ill patient will experience escalating levels of anger. It can begin as disappointment, remorse and even sadness and it continues to deepen. Without any acceptable or equitable answer to their diagnosis, helplessness continues to grow into a fierce relentless anger. At first it is internalized and only seen in brief momentary responses during the denial stage. Anger then becomes consuming and volatile, turning into uncontrolled rage. The anger like moss continues to creep into the spirit of the terminally ill. The calm is interrupted, displaced by this never ending and insatiable anger. It is an intense hostility for everybody and everything enjoying normality. The more the patient thinks on the unchanging facts of their illness the angrier they become. The "why me" questions may not have answers, however they should not be ignored but understood as valid responses to the patient's condition.

The patient doesn't trust anybody or anything. Everyone is responsible for their condition and no one is helping. People have words but their words are fruitless to change what seems inevitable. No matter what they need it is not available when they need it. It is like being in the house of the three bears. Everything is too hot or too cold or too hard or too soft. What you can't rationalize, you internalize and then you criticize. The cause of the illness is the food, or the water is the culprit, or the air and its contaminants are the reason for the illness. It is where we live or what we do as our occupation. Anger expresses the hopelessness and finality of the diagnosis. The patient is feeling the loss of control and the loss of options. Because the diagnosis is terminal, the patient becomes angry because nothing changes the outcome. When everything is said and done, death is still the giant that cannot be defeated.

The patient looks around, sees others who have not

taken care of themselves still enjoying life while they are dying without any relief. The concern of loved ones seems pointless and patronizing, while healthcare professionals are incompetent, cold and uncaring. The patient is looking at life through squinted eyes and speaking through grinding teeth. The incompetence of the people around them to produce a positive change is apparent. The anger is consuming every thought and response of the patient. The patient is living in a pressure cooker that is now a jiggling pot on the stove about to explode. Everyone around them can hear the sizzle and see the steam, knowing if they just cool off, settle down they won't continue to aggravate an already failing system with an uncontrolled explosion.

Anything, everyone and everything has become the cause for their illness. Anger not handled properly will cause the illness to accelerate. Anger causes one to lose hope and mentally causes the body to say "NO' to any opportunity that could possibly enhance the quality of life or turn things around. Often this stage will render the patient hostile with the world and all those who live in it. They can become hostile to any comfort or care that would extend their days. The care givers, family, friends and the medical professionals receive the brunt of their anger, resentment, frustration and sarcasms. Persons, who are well, will provoke and arouse anger along with persons making any accomplishment or moving forward in life. The fact that others are walking in wellness becomes an offense to the terminally ill person. They are angry at the illness, this alien that has taken control of their lives and they transfer the anger to those around them.

Misplaced anger stops the patient from enjoying or celebrating the accomplishments of their children, siblings, peers or friends who are valuable to their lives. They feel as though they have nothing to look forward to and wonder why they have to hear of everyone else's accomplishments. Anger caused by their inability to control the illness has taken over their lives. It isn't that they are people who envy others' success, it is their illness now has taken over their ability to enjoy life. It is in the darkness of their diagnosis, while seeing others' light of hope, that feelings of inequity give place to anger. The anger is due to hopelessness and helplessness. "What can I do about my situation when even the professionals have no hope? Every plan and hope I have has been crushed by this diagnosis. My tomorrows are limited or nonexistent; as a matter of fact they may already be gone." Anger, however also demonstrates the reality and acceptance of the severity of the illness.

Anger is also the response to pain that is relentless and continues to dominate their lives. Pain has become a constant companion in the illness. Often the medicines given only take the edge off but they never turn

the pain away. Pain is the constant awareness and reminder of the intruder's presence and aggressive internal maneuvers. What do you do when you don't have
any known avenue of escape? Reality is a bit too real
and the answers you want aren't forthcoming. How can
you give voice to fear without admitting defeat and how
do you fight an opponent who has been announced over
the intercom as the champion in your fight for life. What
is there to be happy about when life is escaping you
daily, seeping out of you uncontrollably on a moment-
by-moment basis.

Being angry at the illness without any release doesn't
gratify and there isn't the option to injure or inflict pain
or to retaliate in any way. Transference of anger from
the illness to the people around you, allows you to fight
with an opponent you can both see and injure. The patient is actually given a victory in some area of his or
her life. However those over whom they have victory are
their family and loved ones, who now become uncomfortable during visits. The patient is angry at what they
do not have: life and time. Everyone else has plenty of
both, with the promise of a hopeful future. Family,
friends and professionals have life and are enjoying it
while the patient is daily losing life. The world will continue enjoying normality of life while theirs is almost
over. The patient doesn't want sympathy or a morato-
rium; they want to live. They want a miraculous healing

and they want the illness invading them to be destroyed. Not all patients will demonstrate or experience this stage of anger, but it does indeed exist among many. Sometimes silence is rage under restraint and harmful to the patient's overall condition physically and emotionally.

From the family and staff's point of view, the anger is burdensome; it greatly contrasts from denial, which is understandable. The reason is that this anger is projected in all directions and into the environment randomly without provocation. You are walking on eggshells not knowing what will set the patient off. Patients will sometimes say, "The medical doctors are just not effective, they seem to not know what tests to request or what diet to prescribe since it continually changes. Why should I continue trusting them to make decisions when they have already said they failed or have given up in defeat?" The medical professionals keep patients too long in the hospital and don't respect their wishes. They constantly change orders without listening to the patient. Nurses are more a target for the patient's anger because they are the immediate attendants. Whatever they touch or whatever they do is just not helpful and only hurtful. They are too familiar or detached, too friendly or too task orientated, they never answer the patient's questions and always have to check with the doctors and never return with answer to the questions asked.

Displaced anger is contagious. It is a reproducing cycle of emotions moving from the patient to the family who are expected to continue the battle outside the room at the nurses' station with the same vengeance as the patient. The family's commitment to keep the fight going evidences their love and commitment to the patient and gives the patient additional artillery to utilize in the battle for the expression of their rage. The moment the nurse leaves the room, the bell rings. The light goes on the very minute they start their report for the next shift. When they fluff the pillows and straighten the bed, they are blamed for never leaving the patient alone and when they do leave the patient alone the light goes on with a request to have the bed made more comfortable. Family and friends respond with grief or tears, guilt or blame and are often brought into the fight with the medical staff. The patient sometimes will question if family members care how they are being treated by the medical staff.

The irony and awkwardness of this stage may be reflected in the hesitancy of the family to visit. They come less frequently or stay for shorter periods of time. The atmosphere of the visits has become tense and changes from supportive to hesitant. It has become a battleground full of displaced emotions and restraint. The patient is not sure how or what they feel and this confusion or uncertainty is displayed in their anger.

They are wrestling with an opponent who is continually gaining the advantage. Family and loved ones are often confused about what to say, do or whether to even come. Visitors are frustrated because they can't put themselves in the patient's place and identify or even absorb why the anger is against them. Visits become brief, strained as family members begin to avoid or miss visits. This will only increase the patient's discomfort, confusion, isolation and anger. This is a familiar scenario for persons who are terminally ill and for their families.

Now the patient is experiencing the loss of relationships caused by their anger; however to the patient, it is another thing the illness is stealing from them. These relationships are essential to the patient's sense of belonging or inclusion in the family and in life. This is a time to regain and not to lose. Those who demonstrate "Presence" must be careful not to get caught up in or offended by misplaced anger. We must find a way to distance ourselves from the anger, yet not from the patient. Our absence would just be another area of frustration and loneliness the illness has brought to the patient. The patient and the family need our presence as they adjust to the illness and reaction. Expecting this reaction however, doesn't make you resistant to the attack.

This is also a time when we can effectively assist the family, loved ones and even the professionals. "Presence" can bring reconciliation in the place of anger, hurt, confusion, isolation and futility. We affirm the importance of the family to the patient's well being and understand their reactions. We remind them that this is the illness responding and not the person they love and know. We talk with professional care givers, reminding them of their basic skills in these areas of patient responses. When possible we are with the family for their comfort, persistence, peace and healing. We encourage them by reminding them how essential their presence is to the patient and that no one can ever take their place. We understand they also may be building a wall to help them through this illness by avoidance.

We help them understand the anger of the patient; we would be angry if all our life activities were interrupted so prematurely. We would feel resentment if all the projects we started were to go unfinished or completed with changes, by someone else. We would also feel bitterness if we had to scrimp and save money for travel, for retirement and the pursuit of hobbies in our later years, only to learn, "this is not for me." If we had dreams and visions of great changes and improvements for society as a whole and struggled a lifetime for major financial security which now is within reach, only to learn that life is ending; we too would be angry. It would be as if we had lived in vain. What else could we do with our anger, but release it on the people who are most likely enjoying what we are losing. Persons who have ordered unpleasant tests and prolonged hospital stays with great cost and restrictions will go home at the end of the day to enjoy their lives, but the patient, for the most part, is forgotten.

For the patient frustration builds as they hear, "lie still so that the infusion or transfusion does not have to be restarted," or "this will pinch a little." At this point, the patient may feel like jumping out of their skin or doing something to evidence they are still functioning on some level and not for someone else's convenience. The patient experiences the futility and irony of continuing tests and treatments when they have already received the final report. It seems that everything in the environment incites anger. Facing death and feeling life slip away daily are legitimate reasons for anger. It is certainly no laughing matter. When a patient overhears joyous laughter by persons in the hall outside the room while they are dying and in pain, it is absurd to them. The patient may feel anger because there isn't anything laughable about their circumstance.

The patient expressing anger is the person who was in control of his life before the terminal illness. This patient is angered by the fact that they no longer have control and can't affect the prognosis or stop the imminent end. When control is lost, anger is found. The patient is now rendered defenseless, vulnerable and filled with a toxic mixture of emotions. During this state of anger, emotions run high for the patient, the patient's family and friends. This stage can be seen clearly and is exemplified by the business executive, the professional, the entrepreneur, the handyman, the head of household who have all made a career of being in charge and maintaining control of any and all situations. How do they now relinquish control to this enemy invader?

In the ministry of "Presence" we don't have to bring reason to every unreasonable thought or feeling. **We cannot attempt to bring our sense of order to the disorder and chaos of terminal illness. We can help in understanding the validity of the anger and not allow it to discourage us from continuing to be available and helpful.** When possible we can help by redirecting the anger to a positive rather than a negative. Allow the anger to help the patient accomplish a victory in some area to have control no matter how brief that control may last. Then celebrate the victory with them. Gently remind the patient they may well be aggravating or giving the illness an advantage through their anger. Allow the patient to vent and encourage them to talk it out so they don't internalize the anger. We can be a good energy for the comatose patient, speaking calm reassuring words, so peace can enter into a quiet troubled soul, reminding them of the *one* who is in the battle with them.

In the ministry of "Presence," one is always aware of the body, the mind and the soul being under the attack of illness. The patient is reacting to an enemy invasion and we must help amass a strategy to help them to have as much quality and hope as they can in their current life condition. We are always sensitive to the rigors of the illness and the toll they take on the spirit of the terminally ill. We cannot measure patience with a short stick but we must maintain an active and committed prayer life to help us endure anger and resentment. It is not personal although it is personally directed at those around the patient. Often you may have to maintain the peace and assurance of family, friends, caretakers and even medical professionals. Your "Presence" is the presence of the *one* who will never leave or forsake any of the parties involved.

"Presence" insures that everyone involved is under God's care and that He is still presiding over the affairs of men even when we don't understand His current activity. Our presence reminds the family that they are the most important and necessary part of the patients fight to live and helps the family fight for the life of their loved ones without fighting the loved one. We represent the patient under fire with resolve and without inflicting additional wounds to the already wounded. "Presence" kneads knowledge into compassion and applies it gently and with confidence to the wounds and helps to bring light to dispel the darkness.

Exercising the gift of
listening and speaking
can bring the terminally ill
to disclosure,
acceptance of forgiveness
and most importantly
self-forgiveness.

Chapter 4

THE TERMINAL MANEUVERS

$\mathcal{A}$lmost every city has a flea market or swap meet where people go to get bargains and unusual items. We gas up our cars, traveling to some far place, making a day trip of it so we can bargain for the purchase of the products we want. We stroll down the aisles, looking for the right prices. Once we settle on our desired items, we see the asking price and then the process begins. We take that price as a suggested price and the place to start our negotiations. Just as the woman whose car I bought, bargained for the price she wanted and I for what I wanted to pay, we are accustomed to bartering for what we desire. The desired goal is for both parties to come to an equitable and satisfying buying resolution, where both the seller and the buyer are pleased with the negotiation process. It has become a win-win situation for both parties. Even if I do not always get the exactly negotiated price I do not expect to pay the full asking price either.

My wife is an expert at bartering and negotiating to get the best price for a quality item. She can out wait and out negotiate the best salesperson when it comes to purchasing her desired item. She will make periodic visits to view the item with a raised eyebrow to keep the seller aware of her continued interest. She is going to out wait the seller and not give into the asking price. She is satisfied with the quality and craftsmanship of the item but the price is always negotiable. She will refuse to purchase a lesser item but will with patience, practical and pleasant negotiations and repeated visits wear out the seller. I often rely upon her skills to obtain the prize and not compromise the bottom line of spending.

So it is with the terminally ill in the stage of illness bargaining. It is exemplified by the statement, "Let's make a deal!" The patient, as a way of accepting the illness, will begin to express their feelings with statement such as: "Maybe I can make a deal with God," or "maybe He will grant me six more months beyond my predicted prognosis," or "maybe God will allow me six more months beyond my predicted prognosis," or "maybe He will allow me to escape the intense pain and allow me to slip away peacefully." This is a common negotiation stage among patients, particularly those who have some allegiance to a Divine Creator. It is the final appeal to the *higher* court for leniency or mercy. I will appeal my case to God for a righteous and acceptable resolution. I may even ask Him to review my life record to support my claim for leniency.

This bargaining is a very private issue, kept far away

from family and friends. The patient will not reveal his one line bargaining to anyone. Once in awhile, a patient will break the confidence code surrounding the bargaining process, to share it only with the clergy who represent ministry. This may only occur because the clergy is seen as an extension or assistant of God. Therefore they are soliciting inside intervention or a life advocate for their cause. The cause of course is an extension benefit to prolong life expectancy. We never want to lose sight of the fact that a terminally ill person is fighting a life fight and he or she does not want to lose. Death is not a convenient or sought out resolution to the illness that has come upon them. They want a divine intervention and the positive effect of continued life. In simple terms the patient wants to continue to live and not die.

"PRESENCE" takes note that not only is the patient's physical body under attack, but for those who are faith focused they may at this time be losing the faith that once was their focal point, completed them and made them enduring. After all their faith is taking a beating as the question of God's faithfulness is being challenged by the sickness. They are facing the dilemma of inequity and God's unresponsiveness. How can a good God who knows my faith, now desert me in a time when I need Him most? I am Moses, Pharaoh is behind me, the "Red Sea" before me and I need a rod or at the least some help in getting my troops across the sea. The terminally ill are in a faith crisis and bargaining with God like Hezekiah, seems like an equitable and reasonable course of action. Just a few more days, months and even years is all they are asking. Review my record and find the loophole or small print that will allow me to continue life as I know it.

Most of us are familiar with these bargaining terms, especially in a child and parent relationship. The child bargains with the parent differently at different stages of life. A typical scenario for a young child is the promise to go right to sleep if they can stay up late. The teen will offer to wash the dishes, take out trash or sweep the floor with the expectations that the parent will rescind a previous directive. Of course if they are denied their request the bargaining changes to doing some extra chores. The urgency of the request continues to become more penetrating to include the all time famous line, *"if you let me have the car tonight, I won't drive it on the weekend,"* as if the weekend driving was even on the table or an open option. We have become accustomed to negotiating, bargaining for the best advantage and the winning, at an early age. There are no finalities, no cut off dates; all things are subject to negotiations.

Another example of people negotiating is the person who is sentenced by the court to be imprisoned, who strives to be a model prisoner. This effort to be a paragon of virtue is motivated by the expressed desire to reduce the original sentence leading to an early release. Even an inmate sentenced to death row can begin the process of plea bargaining to reverse the sentence from death to life without parole. A student who failed to do the original assignment is looking for a makeup project to insure they pass the grade. Or the employee, who is late coming to work, wants to offset their lateness by coming in early the next day. The husband, who forgot an important anniversary date, is now at the jewelry store hoping to convince his wife that it was his plan all along to purchase a gift for her. At some point we have used bargaining to accomplish our desired goal.

The terminally ill patient uses the same maneuvers, tools and strategies to cope with the present reality. They know from past experiences, that there may be a slim chance that they may be rewarded for good behavior and granted a wish for special services. The wish is most often an extension of life, followed by the wish for a few days without pain or physical discomfort. The patient will many times accept the forecast of the medical doctors and prognosis hoping to appeal it with God who is the "higher power." The patient has a bargaining option on the table listing their services if the extension is granted. The patient is not trying to avoid death or cancel death, but only seeking to defer death's immediacy. They make reasonable and sensible requests for what appears as an untimely execution for a crime they didn't commit. The patient is attempting to arbitrate their way out of what is an unfair judgment or sentence.

Some arbitration arguments include: *"Lord let me live long enough to see my children become adults."* Another is, *"let me live long enough to see my first grandchild."* Still other requests include adding years to one's life, while others ask for special moments before the end. These requests include living to see one's favorite team win the series, or finishing a life project they have been working on, or selling the house, or paying up the mortgage or simply to eat a favorite meal without digestive problems. Allow me to embrace my loved ones before falling into an eternal sleep and whispering, "see you on the other side." It all adds up to a life extension, a life accomplishment being fulfilled or at least having control on the outcome.

The patient who is participating in bargaining has accepted the terminal illness. They are no longer in the denial and anger stages, which is viewed as a positive progression. In acceptance the patient is no longer fighting the diagnosis and is open to explore avenues that may prolong life or at the least defer the inevitable. The patient in the bargaining stage has nothing else to lose; "Why sit we here until we die?" ...*2 Kings 7:3*. There has to be some last option open, a last ditch plan besides just sitting outside the gate waiting to die. The patient is looking for the light at the end of a dark, dismal tunnel or at least a rainbow after the storm. The options may be limited and not without risk, however the hope becomes addition and not subtraction. A few more years or days to complete my life assignment is the plea. Why sit here and willingly surrender without using every available option to live and not die.

Let's exercise any option or possible alternative to simply sitting and watching a clock, which is already draped in black or the hourglass already losing sand. Many times the hope, spark of possibility will be just enough to keep the patient wanting to face another day. It may keep them making important relationship connections and life extension steps. This inner and personal bargaining with God leads the patient into believing, it is not over yet or nothing is impossible with God. This bargaining stage is helpful to the patient who may have lost all hope. This new emergence of hope allows the patient to believe often in what is simply unbelievable or impossible to others. It is in simplicity that the true definition of faith is revealed. Therefore we are careful not to dismiss bargaining because in the process we can disarm faith. In "Presence" we persevere to keep the faith and patient alive to embrace every moment of life.

Most bargains are made with God and are usually kept a secret or implied between the lines of conversation in a chaplain's private office. During an individual interview, it was disclosed that the majority of the requests made to God involve promises: (1) a life dedicated to God (2) a life involved in genuine Christian service in exchange for an opportunity to live longer and (3) a chance to defer death. Some patients have promised to donate parts of their bodies to science, only if the medical professionals promise to use every means available to extend their life. Bargaining is the heart's cry for life and not death; and why not cry out using every tool available to obtain what you genuinely want, an extended life?

Students of human behavior hold that bargaining is directly related to feelings of guilt. This conclusion comes from their experiences in gathering information related to patient disclosures of bargaining. The patient may have been one who did not take time out for church, always hustling, always too busy to establish a genuine relationship with God. The patient, who bargains, may be a parent who did not take enough time to share important moments with their children. Now there are feelings of guilt about taking time out for everybody else's children and not theirs own. These parents may be trying to deal with their guilt first, rather than just trying to prolong life. However my personal experience with terminally ill patients is that bargaining is a natural human response to regain some control of life.

"Presence" speaks to the now of the patient's life and carefully attempts to help the terminally ill navigate from past failures into the moments of today and into faith. The failures of yesterday which we all have can only be resolved in today, since yesterday cannot be changed. Helping the patient with unresolved guilt helps them to live in the power of today and to have some successes today. **Exercising the gift of listening and speaking can bring the terminally ill to disclosure, acceptance of forgiveness and most importantly self-forgiveness.** This will lead to an immediate release of illness inhibitors, which can be seen in the peace that it brings to the patient. This peace is an absence of the internal conflicts that worsen the existing condition. Although bargaining can be viewed as unrealistic it can also be seen as relational and faith-based. Some of the key elements of successful prayer or negotiations include some form of bargaining for benefits. Whatever the patient is able to realize and receive include some type of bargaining with God.

Depression is a response
of helplessness
or hopelessness;
it is not weakness.

Chapter 5

THE TERMINAL DEPARTURE TIMES

*T*he expected maternal delivery date is a target we are aiming for. Thoughts of the delivery date bring joy, hope and anticipation for the future. The body begins to drastically change to accommodate the growing life within it. In anticipation of the occasion, we have a baby shower so friends and relatives can join in our excitement. We begin fixing up the baby's room to hold all the mounting supplies we will need. Each stage brings a new challenge as the waistline enlarges, the feet and legs swell, the size of the breasts increase and even the appetite changes. The pregnant woman becomes smell sensitive and quite emotional. There is discomfort in the back, excessive loss or retention of fluids. There is expected weight gain, morning sickness and sometimes weight loss. Women often experience hair loss or hair growth. The clothes no longer fit and no one can imagine how this can be the same person. These drastic changes during the pregnancy are expected and though often unpleasant, the end results outweigh the temporal manifestations of the pregnancy.

Along with the physical changes of pregnancy there are dietary changes. Pregnant women cannot tolerate some foods and others contain too much sugar, too much salt and are sometimes too spicy. Physician visits become more regular as the expected delivery date gets closer. The anxiety begins to build and intense preparation for the new arrival becomes apparent. The physiological or mental state of a pregnant woman is that she can go from 0 to 100 without provocation. She can move just as quickly from tears to laughter and back to tears within a few moments. From the time she goes into the doctor's office to get the diagnosis of a pregnancy, she knows exactly what to expect. After all she can find books, blogs or groups that can help her anticipate the few months ahead. Family members look forward to the new addition and a celebration may be planned.

In contrast, a terminal diagnosis leaves one hopeless and of the opinion that there is nothing left to do but to lie down and die. For example, a 31 year old female who undergoes a mastectomy and who always took excellent care of her body, now has feelings of inferiority. The singer or speaker who has lost his or her voice due to throat cancer is overwhelmed with the knowledge that their singing career has ended. The robust construction worker who now has to spend 12 hours a week on dialysis feels useless and weak. This stage of hopelessness and depression can be extremely fatal to the body, mind and spirit. There are many barriers placed before the terminally ill patient. Their mental and physiological responsiveness and how they internalize the facts of the diagnosis can be difficult barriers to cross. The patient may find it extremely difficult to look in the mirror, since what they now see doesn't resemble who they were. Their skin, weight, shape, hair, teeth and often posture have drastically changed. It is extremely hard to encourage one's self when faced with the hard visible realities that now exist.

The term "terminal illness" brings with it the knowledge of an ending without a cure. One might conclude that there is not any immediate breakthrough in research and that their condition is going to deteriorate. As their condition worsens, everyone knows the inevitably is death. The patient feels as though they are watching the clock for an upcoming event and they cannot change the outcome. The problem is although the terminally ill have an expectancy date, it is not a welcomed event. There is no "mind game" one can play that will make the facts of terminal illness acceptable. Death is not the prize or event they want to embrace or consider as reality. The everyday living with the facts of the illness and seeing it take more liberty with their lives can often bring about some depression. **Depression is a response of helplessness or hopelessness; it is not weakness.**

Depression is an additional illness the terminally ill must contend with. It involves the body, frame of mind and affects how the terminally ill eat and sleep. It further affects the way one feels about one's self and the way one thinks abouthis or her situation. It is an overwhelming sadness that permeates every thought and action. Depression goes beyond having a bad day or being in a blue mood. Depression is not a personal weakness or a condition that one can simply wish away. The patient is reacting to life or the lack of hope for life. It is almost impossible for patients to simply pull themselves together and get a positive mindset. They now have another illness contending in the ring with them, taking over their thoughts and responses. Depression is a responsive condition to a very real life situation.

The terminally ill will experience loss of emotional expression, an uncontrollable sadness, anxiety or emptiness, being void of any feelings. They can also become overwhelmed by the feelings of hopelessness, pessimism, guilt, worthlessness, fear and helplessness. They begin to withdraw from daily living becoming uninterested in themselves and their personal condition. They are sometimes tired and want to sleep away the time they have left or they may experience insomnia, early-morning awakening or oversleeping. With depression they have trouble concentrating, remembering or making decisions and can become restless, irritable and have thoughts of suicide. This response is now adding to the original illness and is stealing the life from the patient who is still very alive. It has moved from being a response to being an illness contributor.

The depression is enhanced when family and friends diminish their visits and phone calls. The patient chooses not to smile and is not able to celebrate the high moments in history and yesterday's celebrations. After all, life for them is already over. What do they have to celebrate? They cannot enjoy any benefits of today because the depression has overshadowed today. There are no happy thoughts and certainly no victories that they can appreciate. Why open the curtain to be ridiculed by light, when all around you is obscurity and darkness? The patient who is depressed is not able to seek out any benefits in life and shift into a mode of being thankful for what they still have. The illness has become the victor in all things. They see themselves as the victim in their own assessment and without assistance; they are stuck in this dark place.

When the terminally ill patient can no longer deny their illness and finds they can no longer "smile it off," they may find that the energy to care about what happens to them is no longer present. When the patient begins to have more symptoms or becomes weaker and thinner, the option to "give up" becomes larger than a life extension. The patient is now traveling the highway called depression. The life troops have stopped fighting, have stopped their defensive actions and hopelessness has set in.

Each day the situation worsens as the psychological and physical losses increase. The patient develops a sense of great loss, which is manifested in many ways. Women who must learn to readjust to the changes that their bodies have undergone after the removal of one or both breasts or a hysterectomy are examples of patients who may experience this great sense of loss. The loss extends beyong a physical sense; many women feel that they have lost their femininity. Or consider the singer who is left without vocal cords and teeth after surgery for throat and mouth cancer. Her face, which cannot be hidden, is disfigured. These are examples of the tremendous shock, dismay and the cause of a deep depression.

Extensive treatment and hospitalization can cause financial burdens and compounded depression. The patient is experiencing the loss of luxuries and necessities, which cannot be afforded any longer. The high dollar costs of treatments and hospitalization result in large out of pocket expenditures forcing many patients to sell their possessions. Some patients lose their homes, which were intended for their old age and evidence of life's success. Some are now unable to send a child to college because funds are needed for continual treatment. There may also be the added loss of employment because of absence or the inability to execute the employment responsibilities satisfactorily. Sometimes, the wife becomes the primary provider for the family, depriving the children of parental attention. The husband is greatly affected because of loss of marital intimacy. Husband and wife also experience the loss of companionship and outside social involvement. Depression breeds an overwhelming sense of loss which cannot be recovered.

Any kind of loss, large or small, is reason to feel depressed. I can remember visiting a patient who was in the burn unit of the hospital. The patient had a severe electrical burn. He had been struck with a high voltage of electricity, which traveled through his body causing excruciating pain and damaging parts of his body. Many days I sat with the patient as he waited for surgery. Each time he exited the operating room, he left a part of his body behind. The losses stimulated strong feelings of depression and repulsion. The losses dramatized the realness of his situation. This experience captures the predicament every terminally ill patient faces daily. The illness drains until there isn't anything recognizable left. Former life cannot be resuscitated and they are mourning tomorrow today, instead of living as much as they can.

Regardless of whether the depression is reactive or preparatory, it is a very real enemy of the terminally ill. In reactive depression the patient is responding to a present loss and feeling the weight of the loss. The male who develops gangrene in his leg because of a diabetic problem, now is facing the amputation of the leg and reacting to the process. His depression is in the reality of his loss of limbs, mobility and independence. His depression is for today and he is reacting and responding to what is currently happening. The amputation is a piece of himself that he is losing to the illness, which he is helpless to fight. Even medical professionals cannot control the illness. The personal loss is when the patient can no longer control or even be aware of bodily functions, have been reduced to wearing the garments of a newborn and the patient is now in a reactive depressive state. The losses have become overwhelming and irretrievable, thus rendering the patient hopeless.

Preparatory depression is what the patient experiences and expresses for himself and his loved ones. The father who is dying because of cancer is depressed further because he will not be there to provide for his children, to discipline and share precious moments with his family. The mother with a terminal illness will miss the graduation, weddings and normal events of life. Parents will have to endure the death of a child before their own. The spouse will face overwhelming debt and loss of revenue alone. Most of the family's resources, or the 401K, has been depleted. So what does the patient have as encouragement? These issues are real and the patient starts to prepare for the inevitable. Depression sets in.

There are many signs of depression. Excessive sleeping becomes a coping mechanism for dealing with the current condition. The impending total loss of life supports depression. Sleep has become a mystical get away or momentary escape from the reality of the situation. It has not been documented, but there is a common opinion among the masses that death is easier to face when sleep is an option as opposed to being awake. Often times, seniors will pray, "Lord, take me in my sleep," or "I want to be sleeping when death comes." Sleep is a peaceful haven for many patients experiencing depression. The terminally ill patient is often bombarded with medications, causing genuine reasons for sleep and escalating the probability of depression.

Depression is sometimes viewed as "selling out." This is when the patient loses all hope, reaching a low point and never regains a positive perspective. The patient then falls into the *selling out* category. The patient is on a downward spiral and can only envision doom, gloom and loneliness with no chance of recovery. The patient gives up, makes his last stand and throws in the towel. There are some who will never move beyond the depression stage or the selling out stage. Persons who are experiencing such stages will need companionship that can be sensitive to their needs and provide a *ministry of presence* that will both support and encourage participation in life to those who are still living.

The activity of "PRESENCE" is vitally needed during this adjustment time to recognize and assist the patient, family and medical professionals in promoting a physically and spiritually healthier environment for the patient. The terminally ill cannot be forced out of depression and depending upon the level of depression, medications may be required. However, deliberate encouragement, which can be that gentle touch or the reminder that calls you back to life and interaction, is needed. It is the soft announcement that turns on the lights in the darkness revealing necessary input that is vital in the decisions and interactions of the lives of those who love them. It is the action of inclusion, which when done effectively, thoughtfully, tactfully and with sensitivity, can bring the patient's focus to the importance of life, while there is life.

The deliberateness of "PRESENCE" thoughtfully reminds the terminally ill that they are present in this life now and helps to motivate, with understanding and patience, a return to life today. It brings them back to the place where they can make decisions about what is happening today and have an active involvement in their life. It helps the family and friends to not participate in a depressive episode of their own, keeping their loved one above ground for as long as possible. The inclusionary action helps the family and loved ones not to become reactive or over preparatory in the direction of death, but instead embrace, enjoy and glean in the field of life. The attitude of the family, professionals and ministers must remain consistent—not overly cheerful but intently involved and filled with love, compassion, respect, understanding and hope.

When one is optimistic,
hopeful and faithful,
almost anything is possible,
even total recovery and
going against the odds

Chapter 6

THE WAIT AND WEIGHT
OF ACCEPTANCE

*T*here is a great multiplicity of types and weights of acceptances in our lives. We can accept in joy, with a sense of accomplishment and humility the accolades for a job well done or the rewards of our work. The acceptance when receiving the letter of approval for college, fraternity, sorority or the job of our choice, can bring on anxiety when facing new challenges. There is the acceptance of life's situations or relocation changes due to economics, relational, occupational and transitional changes that are commonly and humanely understood. We learn to live with and accept the changes with their positivity and negativity. We accept unfavorable news, demotions or dismissals with the hope of regaining or diversifying our lives and we struggle to embrace the change. These are just some of the natural acceptances of life and as long as there is life it can be adjusted, reasoned with and altered to fit the new set of normalcy.

Acceptance can be a favorable reception or a temporary nod with the hope of change or improvement. It is easy to walk down the aisle to the cheers of spectators who have gathered to celebrate your accomplishments. You walk down the aisle towards the podium a bit nervous and apprehensive once your name has been publically announced, however there is a joy and a favorable anticipation. It represents a different moment, a change in time or completion of a task to accept a community service award or have a street named after you. I am expected to give an acceptance speech, which includes my appreciation for all the people who made this moment possible and I hope not to forget any of them in my nervousness. There is a mixture of nerves, humility and happiness as I clear my throat moving forward as the cheers are hushed and my speaking begins. As a pastor, lecturer and counselor, I have become accustomed to addressing audiences big and small, however, when sharing with the terminally ill patient, I am confronted with a different set of challenges that sometimes leave me searching for what to say and do.

There is another level of acceptance. It is approval, congratulatory and appreciative. It is not difficult to accept this great outpouring and acclaim. It is very different than the acceptance level that comes when you walk away from the physician who just told you that your illness is terminal. As you walk down the hallways leading from his office, you pass many open doors to vacant rooms that seem to pull you in. These doors lead you to places you don't intentionally want to enter, yet visiting them seems unavoidable. These are doors leading to delays, which steal from the terminally ill patient precious time because they are lowered into rooms filled with denial, anger, negotiation, depression and even faithlessness. These doors are on an automatic opening system as the patient attempts to pass them by. These side rooms beckon the patient to come in appealing to their feelings and coaxing them to use precious time within the walls. Each room is finely constructed in logic, wishes, resentment and remorse but these are time traps which if possible, should be bypassed, have limited access or no access at all. Entering such rooms can be fatal.

Although having a clearer understanding of a process can make it seem less intimidating and provide a sense of more control to the terminally ill patient, terminal illness and its effects are not an exact science. The patient is not going through some predictable process of coming to terms with death. It may not happen this way and we do not have the right to push them toward acceptance as a staging area of death. Although they can be on their way to the stage of acceptance we cannot help them arrive there any sooner. We cannot raise the curtain or put up detour signs. Acceptance is filled with a mixture of emotions and must not be confused with hopelessness. As the patient accepts and begins to adjust to the facts and reality of the illness, the patient begins to stop the internal fight, which weakens natural resistance. Acceptance or acknowledgement is a big step towards making the best of the last days. The patient has not lost faith or hope, but they have stopped the great warring within which weakens them. Pain and disappointment may be there and tears may flow, but the load is not as heavy because everything is out in the open and on the table. In acceptance or acknowledgement, patiens can take some control of the life they are living right now. They are learning to live as fully as possible, while acknowledging the presence of this terminal illness.

Persons such as Michael Landon, Lee Remich, Count Basie, Luther Vandross, Curtis Mayfield, Farrah Fawcett and many others have experienced their last days being full because they accepted or acknowledged their illness. In doing so it allows the patient to maintain a clear understandable relationship with friends and family. In acceptance there is the acknowledgement that what the doctors have said concerning the illness is their best assessment of the condition. Facts become what they are, simply facts. The fact is that medical professionals have come to the end of any known cure or stabilization of the illness. Acceptance is acknowledgement of this fact. Medical professionals do not have any additional help available to prevent the illness from continuing to progress. The acceptance or acknowledgement helps the patient and their family to enjoy and appreciate every moment of life that remains. The acknowledgement allows the spirit to quiet itself and to cease from agitating the condition. The patient can look beyond medical limits and become more faith connected. Some may view this as optimism. **When one is optimistic, almost anything is possible, even total recovery and going against the odds.** The days can be extended and enjoyed. Acknowledgement is a bold step to take for the terminally ill person but necessary for self fulfillment and maximizing the days that are left.

If a patient has had enough time and has been helped in maneuvering and working through the open doors and empty rooms of personal frustrations, when they reach acceptance, there is no depression about their "fate." The patient has not experienced "Utopia," nor has the patient embraced an unrealistic idea or peace about impending death that is almost impossible to achieve. There is an eternal peace and resolve around their present state, which begins to germinate within the soul of the patient. The patient can now express and process their feelings of envy for the living and have a healthy anger at those who will outlive them. They would have mourned the impending loss of so many meaningful persons, places and dreams. They would have contemplated much of what will come and go. It may sound like giving up but it is the realization that allows rest from the great battles of denial, anger, negotiations and depression. It is the place of the still waters where the soul, mind, body and spirit experience peace, rest and revival.

In this place the patient will often become tired and weak. This is a response to the illness and not giving up in defeat. The patient will also have a need to doze off to sleep for brief intervals. This dozing off is different from the need to sleep during times of depression or avoidance. It is also different from the sleep or rest period for relief from pain, discomfort or itching. It is a gradual increasing need to extend the hours of sleep. It is a preparative sleeping but it is void of anxiety. This sleep can be restorative as it provides more attention to the "awake" times. It can be followed by extended periods of alertness and cognitive response. It is not a resigned and hopeless "giving up," a shrugging of the shoulders or sense of "what's the use," or "I just cannot fight it any longer!" The patient who moves to acceptance has discovered inner peace that surpasses all understanding and gains additional strength.

Acceptance should not be mistaken for a happy stage. It can be, for some, almost void of any feelings initially as if pain had gone and the struggle is over. It can also be the time of the initial rest before a long journey. This is a time when family should be at its peak in giving support in their presence. When possible, keep a vigil by your loved one during this time. When the patient is still fighting, struggling, not at ease, this stage of acceptance cannot be experienced. Acknowledgement is for persons who have discovered "inner peace." This inner peace is a confident acceptance that gives credence to their brief sojourn, from the *cradle to the grave*. It is a peace that cannot be explained by the human journey or appropriate answers given to the why questions; but it allows all involved to feel comfortable in knowing God's divine will is at work. This becomes a time of acceptance that is good for the patient and the patient's family.

For those of us who believe in the power and presence of God, this chapter in the life of the terminally ill patient can be managed. The patient and the patient's family are embraced with the assurance of the power and love of God in this stage of the sickness. It is the gentle and stable reminder that there is a power and assurance in our ability to let go and allow God to carry us through what we cannot climb over or handle. A belief in someone greater than medical professionals, hospital administrators and the patient advocacy group often provides help and assistance to the patient and reveals a way through all the challenges associated with the terminal illness. To move from a frightened state of mind and mental anguish, to a place of inner peace and genuine resolve in the face of a terminal illness is priceless for both the patient and the patient's family. Consistent and current updates on the patient's condition help both the patient and the family to move to an even more secure place with acceptance.

The family as well as the patient may be experiencing a faith crisis and the presence of a support team reminds them that they are not alone. Connecting with persons who are members of the faith community, believers, trusting God for the unknown, can be most beneficial to patient and family. The activity that comes out of the faith community, the community of believers, enhances the spiritual and mental health of the patient. They are no longer intimidated with thoughts of loneliness because constant support is provided for the patient. The patient does not have to carry the load of being forgotten and left alone to die. Family is present and members of the faith community provide support for the patient and the patient's family. It is important to assure the patient and the patient's family of God's ability to encourage and give courage during this very difficult and draining time.

It is fundamentally important for the terminally ill patient to comprehend the need for a faith that extends beyond human logic and understanding. The activation of one's faith helps the family to not underestimate or overestimate the miraculous that could occur in the life of the patient. The presence of the family even while feeling ineffective, helpless or powerless can be an important source of strength and comfort for persons who are terminally ill. The family is also fighting their issues of hopelessness, loss, fear and anger. There will be times when listening, waiting, praying, encouraging and patience will need to be extended to the family to give them confidence and hope to be strong for the patient. Encouraging one another with presence and genuine words of comfort and care, continues to demonstrate for the patient that love remains constant and does not waver even in the face of sickness. The patient is affirmed in his or her thoughts for family and friends, knowing that sickness does not diminish love and eternal support.

The definition of acceptance can be expanded to include acknowledgement without the loss of hope and despair. While the patient resigns himself to the medical facts of the illness, in that there is no medicine available to cure them or make them better, they are facing the reality of their medical condition. They are recognizing there isn't any known or additional cure, and medically speaking, they have reached the limit of medical know how and nothing more can be done to change their situation. This type of resignation is a type of acceptance but not without faith. Faith at this point is the adhesive that is holding the ship together, not causing it to splinter into pieces in the midst of the storm.

I visited a patient who had been given only two weeks to live; the patient said, "Pastor, I do not want to die. I love my wife and my family, but what more can I do? I have no other choice; I must accept my situation. I'm going to die soon and that's that!" While this is a medical truth, the desire of every terminally ill patient whether they can articulate it or not is to live. The patient wants to live, to embrace life and not to die. They want to discard the pain, the illness and live out their years and plans in fullness. Although they accept the situation and have resigned themselves to the medical facts, they also very much desire life, faith and hope to the very last moment. This can be a time when they become very open to faith because faith includes facts and still gives hope and confidence in God who can do and often does the impossible.

Many patients who have accepted their terminal illness have resigned themselves to the facts and are seeking to be open, logically and sensibly. This state of acceptance allows one to face death boldly and with dignity. They can put up the white flag to God, surrendering to His will, His power and His determination in the life process, knowing death has not had a victory over them or God. The patient is less rigid, loose, open and in readiness for this next challenge. Based on a developing relationship with the patient and family one can determine how the process of acknowledgement is going. One can measure the level of acceptance and also gauge when hope needs to be infused. To sit at the bedside of the patient and continually keep the patient aware of presence with sensitive touches and inclusion in the conversation whether they are conscious or comatose provides great support to the patient. The more eminent death appears to be, the more touch is reassuring and beneficial to them. Remember, hearing is the last train on the track so continue to speak life, truth and faith. Take the opportunity to give a hand or foot massage for their comfort, being sure it will not aggravate their condition. Even when there is no outward response or indication they are aware of your touch, you can still touch them gently and caringly as those wounded on the battlefield of life. Tend and wrap in love their spiritual and emotional wounds, touch them in a heartfelt communion of comfort, patience, understanding and faith.

As the opportunity presents itself, be a ready listener to hear their concerns. It is important to listen to stories about their life and dreams and that their thoughts and concerns are considered and heard lovingly and not clinically. Never underestimate the value of your presence in listening; even when you feel you are doing nothing, your presence is "HIS" presence. It sends the message, "I am here, I am not leaving you and God is here and He will not allow us to abandon you." You represent and send the message that, "God is seriously concerned about you." The terminally ill patient is not the only concerned party, but the patient's family or care giver is in need of support. The family has to manage the time they have left with their loved one and find a safe place, isolated from the patient, to express their uncertainty, faith challenges, anger and disappointment. Support for both patient and family assumes the position of availability, serving, supporting and sharing in this time of "not knowing when."

As we explore and prepare together we will look critically at the facts, fears and implications related to terminal illnesses to obtain a working definition. Our purpose is to give concern to those who have been classified or have been identified as terminally ill. What support can we give? How can one develop a ministry that will nurture, increase faith in God when one's eyes are slowing closing or been closed for the last three weeks or when muscles are dormant and no stimulation is seen or experienced? The question becomes a literal *"how do you give sight to one who is blind and deliver one who is lost."* We must remind ourselves that we are each other's keepers; therefore we remain committed to the patient, understanding we do not have the option to walk away from the patient.

Historically and practically, very little is being done from the perspective of developing a genuine support group or ministry for the terminally ill. We live in an age where life is being extended regardless of the personal cost, but cures are not forthcoming. This can be seen and defined as more people are living longer with terminal illnesses. The illness has been diagnosed and although no cure is available, the life of the patient is extended and can be supported longer with the illness. In other words, the body is being helped to tolerate the illness for longer periods of time, but not without discomfort physically, emotionally and spiritually. Time is essential because with time there is opportunity. The challenge is to move from passive to aggressive and to do more than just making the terminally ill patient comfortable with the sickness. I think it's wonderful that persons who are prisoners to terminal illnesses can be comfortable and not in unbearable pain, but we can still hear the patient crying out, "I want to be free." Families are processing and addressing this important time without help and support in providing the patient with hope and assurance but when acceptance is fully activated the process is much easier.

We use the phrase "WWJD" (What Would Jesus Do). I believe He would minister salvation, comfort and YES, healing. If God wills, we will see reversals of the illness and physical healings; we will also see healing of the spirit, mind, emotions and restoration of the family. Those who are captives will be released to freedom beyond their expectations. We will see undeniable courage and persistency on the battlefields of life and we will see victory in one form or the other. We will witness battle-field courage which will remind us and seal forever in our being, that we are more than conquerors through *Him who loves us and who never leaves us.*

The challenge of how persons can become rooted and focused in addressing and meeting the needs of the terminally ill segment begins with our acceptance. We must accept the challenge to make a difference to forfeit our comfortable sideline positions and run the race of life with the terminally ill. When we realize the need to position ourselves, to provide emotional and spiritual support for families living on the edge of uncertainty, we become effectual. How can we provide relief and encouragement to those facing death? How do we encourage people in denial and trapped by fear? How do we open up dialog that invites the terminally ill to talk freely about their fears and faith? Sometimes it's easier for the terminally ill to share what they are afraid of and explore it with someone other than a family member. To endure the load of terminal illness, acceptance must be embraced and developed in the mind of the terminally ill patient.

Acceptance knows the facts
and understands there is
no further medical intervention
to change the outcome
of the illness
which is void of comfort.

Chapter 7

THE JOURNEY OF ACCEPTANCE

$\mathcal{H}$ave you ever considered the ability to reason with clarity and precision as a gift from God? We can sort through things, go into thinking places, rooms of logic and reasoning that seem so very right and may or may not have anything to do with the true workings of God. We are cautioned that there is a way seeming right to a man that has a destructive end. Have you ever felt trapped or confined with no way out? Have you ever been stuck in an elevator between floors, banging on doors that will not open and no matter what buttons you push, nothing changes? Have you ever found your-self on a winding road that doesn't seem to lead any-where you really want to go? Have you missed your highway exit and traveled on the longest and most des-olate part of the road in darkness with a declining gas tank? Have you ever been told that you will receive credit for finishing the exam but are unsure of 80% of your answers? There is anxiety, fear, discouragement, futility, sense of failure and hesitancy in all these sce-narios.

I'm sure we have all heard the quote, "Don't become weary in well doing for you shall reap the harvest if you faint not." This is easier said than done. What do you do when the journey is about to end or your destination appears to be final and the ultimate end is death? The big questions start haunting you as you run out of reasonable responses. In order for acceptance to be more than tolerance or a waiting for the final chapter in life, it must move beyond what we can rationalize in our thinking. Sometimes, what we consider the failures of our past, hinder us in hoping for the present and the future. Terminal illness is not one of those life contingencies we look forward to as we go through it. We may have secured long-term illness insurances, which in reality do not prepare our psyche or our hope for terminal illness. We prepare "in case of," hoping it does not become a reality. In fact, we only took the plan because of the small premium rates. There isn't any internal stimulus package to boost or enhance our fortitude or faith midst terminal illness.

I once traveled by car from Arizona to Maryland without taking any significant rest or recreational stops in between. I must confess I didn't enjoy this trip; it was a trip out of necessity and not a vacation. The ride was grueling, to say the least and the miles appeared to get longer rather than shorter at every posting. My wife and I continued to encourage each other along the way, but the ride began to take a toll on us. Little things began to be just a bit annoying the further in the journey we went. The tedium of the white line on the road provided no special joy or sense of accomplishment for us. Once we packed and began the ride, we resigned ourselves to the fact that this was our fate for the next three days regardless of how tedious. We had no other choice; we were stuck in the vehicle and stuck with each other. We began after awhile to show the negative effects of the extended ride in lack of patience, weariness and attitude. Yes, we had estimated correctly, accepted the distance in mileage, the cost in fuel and even set up driving schedules. However, what we could not measure or anticipate was the drain physically, emotionally and spiritually.

When we finally arrived in Maryland, there was relief from our long journey. We were not bubbling over in excitement or happiness; we were too tired to exhibit any of those emotions. The trip had taken its toll on us and we were drained and wearied. We were hungry for something other than roadside meals but too weary to fix anything. We wanted to lie down and stretch our cramped and weary limbs. Even in our discomfort, we both were thankful and realized that there was more life to live. There was another day to look forward to after we rested and another event to overshadow the exhausting ride. We would unpack, refresh and even laugh at the experience as we looked forward to the next day with anticipation, hope and excitement.

In the acceptance of terminal illness there are justifiable feelings of futility and anxiety. **Acceptance knows the facts and understands there is no further medical intervention to change the outcome of the illness which is void of comfort.** You feel that you are going in one direction and there are no turning lanes. You feel that you must follow this route to its end and the finality of the diagnosis. With terminal illness the destination or journey end is not Maryland or some other scenic spot. It is not another new beginning with exciting possibilities and challenges. In many ways it is simply an unpleasant, hopeless and a lifeless ending. Often the prognosis only allows for physicians to make the terminally ill patient as comfortable as possible in the waiting room of life. Sometimes this comfort comes at the expense of quality family time. The patient tolerates the illness and often loses precious relationships. Seeing positives for the patient during the final stages of the terminal illness may seem like counting numbered days without any measurable gain.

Terminal illness has always been a part of the human experience and there are many written historical accounts documenting this. Terminal illness is the medical terminology utilized to describe an active malignant or continuing disease that cannot be cured or adequately treated with the expectation of ending in death. However, we cannot lump illnesses into one cause and effect scenario. We still must individualize the response and effects as they are individualized in patients. There is no way to measure how Mary will respond and how Joseph will tolerate the news. Although the illness has an expected end, which is incurable, faith is still very much on the table. So how do we continue to walk in faith and not defeat when we have been given the, *"surrender the troops"* order? It takes personal courage and determination from the patient to not give up or give in to the illness. It is one of the most courageous fights in life anyone will ever experience or know.

Simply put, the terminal illness experience encompasses facing death not hypothetically but in actuality. The patient facing immediate death has relevant questions requiring genuine answers. They are questions that challenge their faith and some even torment them. The questions can range from, "Why is this happening to me and what did I do that was so awful to merit a death sentence?" to "Why do the righteous suffer?" Authentic ministry cannot turn a deaf or nonresponsive ear to these questions. We must bring "Jehovah Shalom," the God of all peace, into the situation.

It is necessary to develop a communicative understanding of God to overcome the harsh realities of a terminal illness. One might even ask, *"How does God who gives life allow death to terminate life prematurely?"* The general consensus of our population believes that death should only come after a long life has been lived. So it was with Jacob in the Bible. After traveling from disaster to the famine relief of Egypt, he rested in his old age enjoying the presence of his children and his children's children. In his old age, he blessed his twelve sons and grandchildren. After having lived a great and fulfilled life, he prepared himself spiritually for life after this life. He released himself to the deep sleep of death (*Gen. 49:1-28*). This was a beautiful sunset on a full life. This scenario is not always so peaceful for persons who are terminally ill.

Facing death with unanswered questions is a frightening experience even for the faithful. Having the ability to release your mind to sleep through the night when you are unsure about the next day requires "Godly peace." Waking up each day in uncertainty of that day's events is living a true "vapor life" that can only be sustained by the peace that God gives. Contending daily not to release the control and specifics of your life to the aggressiveness of the illness is a constant intimate battle effort. There are no trusted profiles by experts who can provide details of the death, having come back with an eye-witness report from their personal experience. It is definitely unchartered and unfamiliar territory and therefore a challenge to our faith and existence.

A person's understanding of death can be the only hope of relief and fortitude to live and not die before their appointed time. The patient's concepts and under-standing, like most of us, come from many different ex-periences, points of view and information of faith and fables often intertwined in life exposures. Death, no matter when it comes, is an unexpected and immediate occurrence for the patient which requires ministry to the family. The terminally ill patient requires effective, in the trench support, to remain focused and not become intimidated by the day to day reports that medically suggest the patient is not getting better. We must ad-dress the patient's concerns with hope, patience, love and understanding.

We cannot be fearful or limited in knowledge because it is an effective weapon against ignorance. There are historical views and questions that, when understood, will help the patient to anticipate, prepare and navigate to a place of faith. These conversations help to destroy the power of myths and fears in the current living of both the patient and the family. Memories will invade the mind of the terminally ill and their families will and can serve as human warnings and fearful reminders of what others have endured. Although, all questions may not be answered to the satisfaction of the patient they should be heard and addressed. Historically many have considered terminal illness as the natural order of things or simply a common road traveled by most. This may cause the terminally ill to believe they are living in the consequence of personal sin or God's displeasure. This is of little comfort and is certainly not faith inspiring to the patient or their family. Addressing unpleasant thoughts and bringing clarity to misinformation assists the patient in discarding negativity, which can be a breeding ground for doubt and hopelessness.

If the illness is viewed as a consequence of sin or disobedience, then it is considered a judgment from God against the patient. How then is the patient able to release themselves to a God who has already given a negative judgment and has sealed their fate? Remember the conversation of Job's so called friends? Job's life, under their microscopic examination, resulted in his best friends Eliphaz, Bildad and Zophar concluding Job must have sinned (*Job 4:5-11*). Their consensus of thought was that *God is too honorable to allow the death of a just man. Therefore, the situation evidences God's displeasure and chastening.* These men and Job himself went so far off base that God interrupted and reprimanded them (*Job 38:1-41*). Job was a generous man who gave liberally of himself and of his provisions; yet he suffered, being assaulted and stripped of his possessions, family and health. This is often the reality of terminal illness. The patient is left alone on a forsaken hill trying to make sense of their condition and finds themselves struggling with the voices of accusations within and without.

Evil, catastrophe, death and illness are often considered as having a spiritual cause and effect, some type of spiritual misalignment disorder. This may calm the fears of those not terminally ill and self-righteous in their own estimation. They believe if they do well, illness can be avoided; this however does nothing for the patient living with a terminal illness. It implies guilt of some sort on the already over weighted brow of the terminally ill. It doesn't help the natural mind to rationalize what it cannot control. We can make a case for the consequences of human choices, moral or immoral and the results of natural catastrophes because of soul negligence. We can conclude and caution ourselves to do preventive health care in our living for life extension, which is prudent and reasonable. Yet as previously indicated terminal illness can come to the jogger, the health addict, the minister, the children and more. Healthy living and preventative medicines help us to maintain a healthy and armed immune system, which can help us defend our bodies against illness. Yet the terminal illness can still come to those who have exercised caution and care.

There is a needed response to the allegations, "If God is good, then why does He permit evil, illness and even death? If God is in control, why do bad things happen to those who are faithful?" Sin is the culprit seen as contributing to terminal illnesses and diseases throughout the history of civilization. Many have believed if mankind could live in harmony and peace, the manifestation of evil could be forever eliminated from society, thus creating a perfect existence, void of sickness, death and suffering. This could only occur if man could live a life free from chaos and destruction. Of course, this would be the "Utopia" and not the reality. If this Utopia existed here on earth, then it would suffer from an over population explosion. This concept would afford us the opportunity to live above conflict, environmental or catastrophic disorders, accidental injury and infections.

Historically, many believed a particular manifestation of evil in human history to be the source of all evil. It is believed that this evil can be attributed to the cause of terminal illness. We want to generalize the causes and manifestations of evil to a package of things to be avoided. We want it to be within our personal development and under our control. We fail to acknowledge that choice has much to do with the expansion and growth of evil. Sin, which is evil, continues to abound, just as grace also super abounds. Evil or working against the will of God, contributes to the forces of destruction and disharmony, but is not its originator. We cannot generalize the causes and manifestations of evil without realization that the root cause of evil is directly related to freedom of choice. Whatever man decides he must understand that the consequences cannot be avoided, whether good or bad, constructive or destructive.

Therefore a particular manifestation of evil in human history cannot be regarded as the sole source of evil. Man's freedom of choices can become the door of entrance for evil. We can choose to feed or starve what is around us. What we allow, condone, embrace or quietly give our assent to becomes a part of us. Corrupted morals in leadership foster sin and a pervasive evil. Rebellion and corruption among the people who are encouraged by leadership to tolerate or become permissive may promote a fellowship with evil. Yet the evil does not gain entrance through guarded or locked doors. Evil and prevailing sin, which is witnessed by the people, can trickle down from leadership tolerance or lack of censorship, but it is not the originator. At the leadership level injustices are promoted and legislated, yet they are not the cause of evil. All these actions, legislations and characteristics result in evil being personified and promoted, but not originated.

The catastrophes of history, which have been attributed to God punishing humanity, can be understood as the natural and inevitable consequences of man's effort to live outside the rule and authority of God in an insecure and vulnerable existence. Human pride undercuts every noble ambition because mankind refuses to acknowledge the need for God. The pride of man, conflicting with the will of God, often leads man to the path of destruction. Yet mankind still has the right and ability to choose where he puts his foot. Man has personal accountability and freedom of choice; it is called *free will.* God is not some tyrant whose will and laws are irrelevant to the structure and hope of man. God cannot be limited or confined to a natural law or concept; God is greater than that. God transcends the law. God is limitless and boundless in every imaginable way. One is still reminded that God is omnipotent and omniscient. He is outside of the box and cannot be contained or limited to our understanding, actions or reactions of man.

We must conclude that everything God made and does is good even when we cannot explain or can give a logical natural understanding of the occurrence. God is merciful and by His very nature and expression of life, He is the essence of good. The nature of God is the single, irrefutable and unchangeable truth anchored and documented in the Word of God. God saw everything that He made and it was not just good, it was very good. The whole biblical interpretation of life and history rests upon this truth. The creation work, the world finite, the dependent world, a world with a contingent existence, is not evil. Death is not always the punishment for personal sin. The finiteness, dependence and the insufficiency of man's mortal life are facts which are imbedded in God's plan of creation and salvation.

The ways of God must be presented for acceptance by man even when they are not understandable. Even when God's ways are past our ability to search them out, it doesn't mean God is thoughtless or vindictive. We accept God's will with reverence and humility, bowing to the sovereignty of the only true and living God. In one of the most beautiful biblical expositions of the glory and majesty of God, the brevity of man is presented merely as a contrast to the proof of His majesty. "All flesh is grass and all the goodness thereof is as the flowers of the field: The grass withers, the flower fades... but the Word of God shall stand forever." (Isa. 40:6-8) We must conclude that even death and terminal illness are included in the natural order. This is a part of the divine working of God in the world. Death itself does not invalidate the promise (that He will be with us to the end) or the Word of God (*Matthew 28:20b*).

One cannot ignore the works of the Apostle Paul as he focuses on death to illustrate the difference between the majesty of God and the weakness and dependence of mankind. This does not mean a physician's diagnosis of physical death is accepted as the final word regarding the fate and hope of man. Although terminal illness is a part of the natural process of human existence, is not final. We are pitiful men, according to Paul, who declares, "if in this life only we have hope in Christ, we are of all men most miserable" (*1Cor. 15:19*). We are born to live and we also must face the reality of death and it may come in the form of a terminal illness. This is a reality that cannot be avoided, overridden or pushed away to the other side of the plate like an unwanted vegetable. However, death is not the end for those who have established a genuine relationship, with their God and creator. Death can be viewed as the untimely interruption of life to be continued.

The suffering of terminal illnesses, pain and other earth shattering and altering situations are a common thread weaved into life. God has allowed these occurrences. This does not mean He is solely responsible for the issues that may interrupt human life. God cannot be responsible for all the ills and consequences of the choices of mankind. He will not violate man's freedom of choice, whether good or bad. The "why" questions are not simply answered, but they include the reality of choices from many sources effecting the quality and longevity of our living. These choices that have been made may not have been made directly but still effect and affect the world balance and the availability and propagation of evil.

We are people of hope
and we do not always understand
the suffering and the distancing
that comes with
the terminal illness.

Chapter 8

SEEING "ACCEPTANCE" AS THE SUN SETTING

*A*s we traveled the road to Pakenbaru, for eight hours, we experienced the beauty and utter wildness of the rain forest. The vivid colors and songs of life and the struggle to reach our destination were amazing. It was a time of celebration for my brother's wedding in Duri, Indonesia. Raw and natural beauty surrounded and excited us. At first glance the rain forest appeared chaotic and entangled with animals, plants and trees. This seemed to be, in reality, an amazing balance of life. Each tree, vine, insect and plant rightly serves and provides substance and survival to its connecting neighbor. Its life and death are essential to the whole of the forest. The return trip took us up and down towering mountains and through hidden valleys. The mountains were breathtakingly beautiful but also breathtakingly treacherous. We experienced both awe and apprehension in large doses on that road.

On the previous day we had crossed the equator; the line separating the earth into northern and southern hemispheres. One foot firmly planted on one side and the other foot in another hemisphere. My body was weary and yet my spirit was ignited. All along the roadside there were signs of life and death coexisting, not in spite of one another, but because of one another. I was awed by God's perfectness of balance, purpose and provision for humanity. I saw life in its fullness of beginnings, continuance, fortitude and death. I saw with my own eyes that *all things can and do work together for good.* We witnessed episodes of God's works. We saw His presence in 'High Definition'. Yet as much as we enjoyed all that surrounded us, we knew we needed to complete the ride to Pakenbaru before night fall. The road we had to travel was treacherous and with darkness and night fall quickly approaching, we all wanted to reach our destination safely.

Night fall is gradual, and like the rain forest, has an order to it. It is not a sudden absence of light but a gradual overshadowing that becomes the night season. It comes with subtle changes in colors and presence. On many nights, as we have traveled together, we have seen the beauty of nightfall. We have marveled as we witnessed persons sitting huddled by a fireplace enjoying the beauty of a consuming fire. We stopped our busyness of thought and travel to enjoy the sideshow in the beauty of the sunset. All the elements which transformed a complicated change into a scenic beauty, such as spectrums of light, atmospheric changes, natural gasses, cloud formations and earthen particles are unseen by us until night begins to fall. We simply enjoy what is a complicated expression of the end of one thing and the beginning of another.

As a pastor for over twenty seven years, I have experienced great and solemn moments that have transformed and enriched my life. Some people call them "Ah-ha" moments. I have treasured these moments which have given me great joy, peace and confirmation to fully embrace my calling as pastor and teacher. I have seen the preciousness of the newness of life and the preciousness of the transition of life. I have also seen the courageous fight for life in the terminally ill. There have been great moments of surpassing joy as persons have given birth to purpose just as fruit ripened on well nurtured vines. I have also witnessed persons push through adversity, as strong vines. They continue to climb over obstacles set in their way. I have seen those who resisted and fought against enemy invaders, even unto death. I have experienced those who have awakened out of the sleep of indifference to become people who make a difference. I have seen a litany of amazing miracles that have reminded me of the awesomeness of God in human lives.

The pastor is called to feed the sheep, even if the sheep do not want to be fed and even those who can no longer sustain regular nourishment. That person who is constantly providing genuine encouragement not only sets the food before them, but will often take up the spoon to help them receive the nourishment needed. We insure that the necessary work is being done to help persons who are terminally ill, to be filled with the life of Christ and confidence of eternal life. To accomplish this, we prepare, disciple and train those who will with diligence continue in the work of sharing with the terminally ill. The world will know the love of God as it is demonstrated to the terminally ill and as we give authentically to one another. We need each other to survive. Our strength is not in our ability to perform but is in our submission to serve and love unconditionally.

We are helpers of one another and we serve one another. In our communion services, it is important that every member serves another. As we pass the elements of the bread and the wine, the membership is continually reminded that we are not to serve ourselves but to serve one another. The communion is a time of unity as we serve one another remembering He who served us all, even unto death. It is so easy to forget the simplicity and power of service in a self-serving world. Every member is an important member and those that appear to be the weakest are often the silent warriors in our midst. Every situation of life is a ministry learning tool. So to continue in serving one another as we provide assistance to the terminally ill is a continuation of the communion outside the doors of the church.

"Leave no man behind," the unspoken code of the

military should also be the unsung song of the ministry of "Presence." There is never a time when assistance is needed more, then when the invasion of terminal illness is present. When weakened by the rigors and despair of terminal illness in our midst the army of the faithful should arise. The patient who is terminally ill is a part of us; they are in pain and under attack and we are compelled to help. Like the white blood cells in our bodies that serve as an army chasing invaders and rushing to the site of the injury to do what is needed to support the body, so we too must rush to the site of injury and faithfully carry and support our comrades during the battle for life.

In 1869 Frances J. Crosby released a mission song entitled "Rescue the Perishing." The refrain of this song simply says. *"Rescue the perishing, care for the dying, Jesus is merciful, Jesus will save."* As people of faith we make Him visible in His saving power not through our invisibility. We cannot be found running around the ship screaming at the top of our lungs in uncertainty. Where is our help, calm assurance and patience needed other than at the bedside of the terminally ill? It's not always enough to wait until the storm passes and then come with our casserole dishes in hand to comfort those who remain. It is important and commendable to aid what remains after the storm; being there to rebuild, fortify and comfort has its place in the overall recovery relief. Yet the totality of work should not only be seen in our post traumatic relief plans but in our effective presence of comfort while the storm is yet raging.

I love the picture of the storm chaser who engages the storm. Those men and women who go out in the midst of the storm to chart its course and to rescue are brave. The deer, who in spite of the danger, is so thirsty that he braves the unknown for one sip of the cool water facinates me as well. In national news, sometimes we can recall the heroic pictures of ordinary citizens who volunteered and risked their lives, without thought, to pull someone off the rooftop or they took their boats to the place of rescue in the wake of a Katrina event. We can recall the pictures of the many rescues from the April 1995 Oklahoma City bombing and the 9/11 bombing of the Twin Towers. Those who rushed into the burning, exploding or crumbling buildings to help deliver those trappedhelped to save lives. Their courageous presence in the midst of what was a present catastrophe was the difference between life and death, hope and hopelessness, for what could not be rescued could be sustained until additional help came. In a crisis based ministry we must always be available and responsive to the terminally ill. It is a life in personal crisis and our presence and assistance is essential.

Before we can begin to plan a program or train in readiness for service, it is important to first become sensitive to the need and informed of the clinical diagnosis so we are aware of the possible hindrances one may face. Providing genuine support is not a clinical adaptation of facts and stages which may be applicable to the patient's condition, but it takes that clinical information and utilizes it as a wonderful tool to establish effectual help for the terminally ill person, their family, friends and medical providers. It should not only bring physical help, but should produce for all connected to this season of transition, love, joy, peace, longsuffering, gentleness, goodness, faith, meekness and temperance. It is a life line to those who are struggling with terminal illness.

There was a commercial some years back about a watch that could take a licking and it would remain operational. It is only through the manifestation of authentic and bona fide love in our lives that one is able to help the terminally ill to keep kicking and to keep ticking in spite of a dismal prognosis. Connection is everything for the power of recovery and for perseverance to be infused into the patient. For the patient to be sustained at a reasonable level of hope, the patient has to possess an indisputable relationship with God. We help them to know they are not alone in their hour of warfare and acceptance. It is imperative that we remain present on the good days as well as on the not so good days. We continue to hear and respect their words, thoughts and desires. We are with them in spirit, which is intangible and we are with them in the physical, which is tangible.

The "Presence" we provide is to the activity of the spirit; it is fueled by being thoughtful, available and informed. This is not the time to engage in arguments of faith, but to reassure and insure that the patient is aware of the love of God in Christ. Psalms 23:6 reminds us that *goodness and mercy shall follow us all the days of our lives.* In a very real and visible way, to demonstrate the fulfillment of this promise, it is evidenced, in the valley and the shadow of impending death. Just as in the journey to Pakenbaru, we could see the darkness approaching, so it is also with the terminally ill patient who is seeing an approaching darkness called death. It is easier to experience the assurance of God's presence and to hope in God on sunny days.

In the midday, when traveling back from Pakenbaru, it is much easier to enjoy the trip. Likewise, when you know the day is ending and darkness of night is approaching, it becomes more difficult to encourage yourself. The beauty of the trip may get lost in the darkness. God is invisible in form and shape, invisible to the natural eye. The terminally ill patient desperately needs to see us when they cannot see or understand Him. Remember we are not God's defense attorney for He has no need of one. We do not defend His actions or what may appear to be a lack of action. Sometimes the patient needs to vent and they also need a simple listening ear. Listen with care and hear the complaints and woes. The goodness and greatness of God, like water, will find its own level in our response and will evidence as we share carefully with the terminally ill. Don't try to explain what is unexplainable for it can only be received in faith.

The "Presence" that is extended to the patient should always be focused and consistent when embracing and sharing with the terminally ill patient. We cannot deny the actuality of the illness or desert the patient when they are unable to communicate. Our best contribution to the patient is when we remain with the patient all the way through the process. It is a life journey from this life to the next. Attachment will become stronger as one continues to share with the patient. **We are people of hope and we do not always understand the suffering and the distancing that comes with the terminal illness.** Our prayers and genuine fellowship must be complete and secure for optimal support for the terminally ill patient during the illness. We must strengthen ourselves in the Word of God as we need to be ministered to in the fellowship of others as much as we need to minister to the patient. This is a pastoral warning to you; you will not go through this time and be untouched. Stay connected to your pastors, ministry leaders and others grounded persons who can help give you the strength and help fortify you during this time.

Visit when you have quality time to spend with the individual. Don't rush in and rush out thinking it won't be noticed. People often notice when others seem to be preoccupied with time. Glancing at your watch or a cell phone to check the time indicates that visitors have more important tasks to which they must attend. Time is more precious to the terminally ill than we can imagine. Once the terminally ill patient has accepted the limits of time, it is invaluable. It is simply bad manners to fit only a few minutes with them in your busy schedule. They will start to feel that they are a burden that no one has time for. The day that you rush in and intend to rush out, just may be the day when they require time to share. Be straight forward. If you really are stopping by on your way somewhere else but had an overwhelming urge to see them, tell them so. It is both honest and still evidences their importance to you. We are in a relationship with the terminally ill and more importantly they are in a relationship with you. Our desire to spend time with them demonstrates caring and validates their importance. We make ourselves available as sincere persons demonstrating love and care to the patient and their family. The patient is the recipient of both.

The trip to Indonesia, like the road trip from Arizona, was a long and grueling trip. We were committed to the trip, but that did not mean that we didn't become exhausted and weary along the way. Sometimes being confined in one place for long periods of time will take its toll. Like being on the plane for twelve or more hours or stuck in the car for two or more days, there is nowhere else to go. If a simple traffic delay or roadside repair changes our attitude for the entire day, laboring with the terminally ill patient can drain us as well. We will need rest emotionally, physically and spiritually to continue. Honesty with God and yourself is vital; you are not superman or superwoman. If you are the primary care provider, take the cape off and take a nap. Visit friends or simply relax with some music. It is important that you don't become ill, depressed or despondent as you serve and assist the terminally ill patient.

While visiting the patient, remember, we are not there to entertain the patient so you don't have to keep a running conversation. Be ready and open to hear. When you speak, let your words be thoughtful, meaningful and not rehearsed, but full of genuine care. When you don't know what to say, don't say anything; don't stop listening. Listen to what is not being said, listen to the change in breathing and listen to complaints without defense. Simply listen to their life story, sometimes told through tears, sometimes through sighs of remembrances and anger due to unrealized hope. Touching is vital but it must be sensitive and not intrusive or sudden, but thoughtful, sensitive and comforting. Look for the welcome signs and avoid helping without permission or invitation from the patient.

On the road to Pakenbaru we gave few instructions to the driver of the vehicle because we were in an unfamiliar territory. We knew general things like the sun rises in the east and sets in the west. This is a fact wherever you are, but we certainly could not navigate our way through the countryside, over the mountains or even through the rain forest. We were passengers in the vehicle, along for the ride, unable to offer help with directions and certainly we could not help with the driving. The same is true with our presence with the terminally ill. We are traveling on uncharted roads and we can only ride with them on their journey. We are companions on this journey with them. As such, we are not the self appointed experts on all they are experiencing.

It is good to understudy before you take a solo flight. As you begin in this journey of sharing and supporting the terminally ill, it is good to begin going with someone who has already traveled this way and has the experience. It is good to understudy and to receive first hand training in order to be the best you can be in preparation to share with the terminally ill. Remember, it is not necessary to announce you are in training to the patient. No one wants a novice walking with them, not even the terminally ill. Visitation and observation are good teachers. Watching, listening and learning all you can from others who are proven in the area of providing "presence to the terminally ill" is very helpful. Be attentive and ready to hear more than you verbalize. Ask thoughtful questions, not the same questions over and over. The terminally ill patient doesn't need to instruct you in what they need or make you comfortable with their illness. The answers to questions or even statements by the patient can be calming and comforting for the patient. Everyone wants to know their words are important and have been heard and remembered, especially those who may be speaking for the last time. Touch the patient if they are comfortable being touched. Speak with clarity and listen carefully so you know what to talk about.

Everyone does not suffer in silence and there are often unpleasant moments and occasions. Remember, nothing you experience can be compared to what the patient is enduring. We cannot tell them how to react to what you have not experienced or to their own physical or emotional pain. If the patient is having a bad day, don't leave. Sit quietly and visit in gentle quietness. If the patient is comatose, it doesn't mean they don't know you are there; visit with them anyway. Talk a bit about things they may have previously said and can recall. Read quietly to them or sing quietly. Let your words be reassuring and comforting as if you expect at any moment they will respond to you. How you look is important; dress pleasantly and leave your weariness outside; come in with a revived and fresh spirit. If you had a bad day, pray before you visit. Take those few moments you need for a personal revival in prayer because at the end of the visit you will probably go home pain free to rest and live to see another day.

The whole purpose of your visit is keeping God present with the terminally ill patient through your presence. In Psalm 121:3-4, God never slumbers and He never sleeps. In other words, He is always awake and aware of our needs; He is our keeper. We bring His presence into the room of the patient. The time of "church going" may be over for the patient or they may have never experienced it, but it is your job to bring the essence of what fellowship is to them. During the visit we certainly don't want to talk about what they are missing but we want to comfort them, for they are members of the extended family of God. We don't ever want to discuss problems but we only want to discuss the things that give hope and provide a calm and peaceful environment. As much as possible, allow the patient to direct the course of the conversation. If they are unable to converse, we still maintain a fellowship attitude in the conversation. After all, no one wants to be treated as a MIA (missing in action) while they are still present and alive.

As a pastor, I carry each member in my heart with

the special love God has given me as a *"under shep-herd."* I, like Him, do not want to lose any sheep that God has entrusted in my care. I watch over the ministry, often times refreshing and reviving those who share in "PRESENCE." During the decline of the health in persons, it is very important to me that immediate support is given. I believe no one should have to carry the load of terminal illness alone. I will visit with the terminally ill and their family as often as I can. I will reinforce my confidence in those who share regularly with them and will keep lines of communication open. I will effectively train those who will also take the daily oversight for this responsibility. These individuals are my eyes, ears, hands and my heart, caring for and being attentive to persons connected to the family. They will keep in close communication, keeping me abreast of any changes in the condition of the patient, any issues of the family and any pastoral needs anyone may have. We work as a team which benefits the terminally ill and their family.

Through the paradigm
of presence,
a caregiver or
one who is deeply concerned
about the patient
can provide immediate
and sometimes silent
support to the patient.

Chapter 9

THE HOW, WHAT AND WHY
OF ACCEPTANCE

*I*n providing support to the terminally ill I have come to know the importance of the exchange of ideas and thoughts. It is important and it keeps what I am called to do for the terminally ill fresh, meaningful and relevant. Our intentions and efforts are to develop a relationship dedicated to addressing the total needs and concerns of the terminally ill and their family. Not only do we not want to leave persons behind, we also don't want to leave them alone on the battlefield of sickness. It isn't enough to simply call for the medic in the midst of the crisis, but it is also important to provide the continual care that can only be adequately expressed through someone who genuinely cares rather than by persons who are compelled to go out of personal guilt. We are the support soldiers to the terminally ill. And as such, we reach out in every area of need. A clear definition of our mission and mission field will be *home missions*. We are made to be interdependent as a body. No one man is that island to himself or herself. Support and care to others is always needed.

In the healthcare system we are known to have a primary care physician and specialty care physicians.

When a physician admits a patient to the hospital, the physician will make periodic hospital visits. It is the continual care team, including the nursing staff, which is responsible for the daily care of the patient. The same is true with our family members and loved ones who are terminally ill. The *Chief Physician* has given the orders and we, as the continual care staff, are responsible for providing the prescribed care to the patient. When we are told to love one another, it is not a theoretic or a poetic term of endearment. Love, in its noun form, means attraction or a benevolent concern. But in its verb form, we intentionally demonstrate the action or the activity of love to the terminally ill person. The support we give to the terminally ill and their families is the demonstration as an unselfish love, to serve the one in great need when others are deliberately detaching themselves.

History shows that we have always been confronted with illnesses, thought to be perplexing and incurable by science and medicine. These illnesses range from Lou Garrick's disease, cancer, diabetes, lupus, Acquired Immune Deficiency Syndrome, dementia, Alzheimer's and others. We are continually discovering more virulent strains of viruses and diseases that are weakening our immune system.

What can mortal man do to encourage persons who are given a negative report? How can one give hope to a person who is caught in death's iron grip? How does one provide hope when everyone else is leaning and pointing to death as the conclusion of the matter of life? When given a prognosis that is terminal, the care giver is then faced with a worthy challenge. We are challenged to develop viable support, to encourage, inspire and foster a genuine bond with the terminally ill patient.

Chaplains, as well as general workers at hospitals and hospices to whom I have spoken and worked alongside, have their own set of useful tools in facing this challenge of providing care. Although each person was extremely helpful in sharing activities done with the terminally ill patient, there was not anything written to document the "how to" of their activities. My approach became, "Teach me, show me and share with me what you know and how you were able to effectively initiate meaningful service to the terminally ill patients." As a concerned caregiver to persons who are challenged with terminal illness, the desired direction is to make a genuine contribution that would remind patients that they are not alone in the struggle for a life of dignity. Even if the outcome is not what is desired, they still have dignity and transition in peace. My studies, my research and my experiences focused on information and methods that would give me the tools necessary to achieve this end.

Many with whom I have worked over the years, were open, accommodating and helpful in giving me an overview of their work. These professionals included psychologists, counselors, chaplains and hospice workers. They had many experiences both positive and negative in their approach to effective assistance to the terminally ill. Often one is able to discover what is effective by eliminating what doesn't work. It is an objective look to determine the most productive way to meet the patient at their point of immediate need. In sharing with the terminally ill over the years, I have found a direct connection and coalition to the trial and error method of many professionals. However, I have more importantly found the more progressive a society becomes the more inhumane it can become to areas that are painful and uncomfortable. As we have become more exposed to the terminally ill, we have also become less affected by the plight of terminal illness. We become desensitized by our exposure and familiarity. This regretfully can make us ineffective in our response. Inhumane is not always maltreatment or neglect; it can be desensitized treatment that may even include housing the terminally ill while making them comfortable until the inevitable transpires.

From a learning standpoint my interaction with other professions has been exciting, informative and a positive learning experience. I received a step by step explanation of how their efforts and methods work. This information ranged from holding a patient's hand to giving assurance and support through contact, to providing the same assurance to the family. All of us had a common denominator and that was to assist and help the patient. All of us were seeking to provide a type of effective service to the terminally ill. I found that a clinical overview in being present was the theme of most or all the participants. It was as if we were all on the same journey with different methods of transportation. Some were the quick jets, others the stop and start shuttles, while still others took the train with turns and twists. When I interacted with different agencies I became better equipped to improve and effectively assist the terminally ill.

Through the paradigm of presence, a caregiver or one who is deeply concerned about the patient can provide immediate and sometimes silent support to the patient. The value of presence, being there, is something that is an immeasurable tangible, yet it is an intangible gift to the terminally ill. Presence reminds the patient that life is still available amidst a dismal prognosis. Through this active sharing, the patient is comforted and comes to know that the caregiver has made the patient a priority, despite all other responsibilities. Rather than the patient feeling hopeless, the patient is inspired to fight the "good fight" all the way to the final round. We cannot promise the continuation of their physical life, but we can walk with them in this life. It allows the patient to experience the assurance to know that they are not alone.

All caregivers and loving family members are not medical practitioners, but they can assist the patient in complying with the physician's instruction. As persons who deeply care for the patient they are committed to making whatever days they have left, their best days. Most agencies although effective in the services, usually do not address all of the concerns of the patient. Caregivers who are equipped with the understanding of *presence* can pick up where the medical professionals and other agencies leave off. The questions asked are usually from a servant's posture of "what can we do to make things comfortable for you?" The greatest comfort to the terminally ill patient is in knowing that someone genuinely cares. They need to know that they are not discarded as hopeless.

The 23rd Psalm is one of the best read and rehearsed psalms. It is often used to comfort in the death of a loved one. However, in the ears of the living, David familiarizes us with God whom he refers to as "our shepherd." It is because of Him I can live life fulfilled. David says, "He makes me lie down in a flourishing place and He leads me beside quiet and refreshing streams. He restores, heals and refreshes my soul and leads me in paths of gentleness that is void of condemnation." It is not just one path, but there are many paths that lead to Him.

Participating in the constant and continuous support to the terminally ill requires one to be fruitful and exemplify extreme patience. As one who is called to serve, we need to be sensitive to the patient's total reactions.

Depending upon the patient's medical condition, communication is done in a variety of ways. The patient may communicate by a squeeze of the hand, a nod of the head, a tear falling softly from the cheek or just a facial expression. Other patients may engage in dialogue that will include questions and answers. Others may express anger and hostility. All of these communications, gestures, reactions and questions are just a few of the ways by which the patient responds. This is a time when the patient is not open to long speeches or theological dissertations. Visitors often become overpowering in a crowded hospital room with chattering conversations among each other. It is a time when sensitivity to the patient's needs and expressions is definitely needed.

Patients may sometimes desire the tranquility of a quiet stream or a visit from the one person who can provide a *"Presence of Peace,"* which can be preferred over a room full of visitors. If there is a consistency of visiting, it will reassure the patient of the importance of their life. However a bedside family reunion may well leave behind the breadcrumbs of "I guess I won't last too much longer" in the patient's mind.

Terminal illness includes loneliness and isolation. A

genuine presence, whether from a friend or stranger, is appreciated. Does this mean there should not be days without visitors? The answer is no. However, the best scenario is that there should not be days void of visitation. Your connection with the family should give them confidence to call sometimes and request a visit from you, as the patient or family desires your presence.

Often times sharing with the patient is composed of three basic components. They are the *what,* the *how* and the *why.* It is not as clinical as it may appear. In the *what, how* and *why,* we can discover and uncover some of the issues that can hinder the patient from being productive and peaceful. As we review the what, the how and why as it relates to the terminally ill, the response of the chaplain may be immediate and personal when providing comfort to the patient.

The *"what"* is interpreted as the need of the patient. What is the need of the patient? Does the terminally ill patient wish to speak with a chaplain concerning their illness? Does the patient desire the presence of someone in the room in dealing with the last few moments of life? Does the patient have something to say or something to release verbally? Does the patient desire a listening ear? The patient must be the first to initiate any visits from the chaplain's office or from the hospice agencies. In order to experience an effective "what," the patient must want or request it. The chaplain doesn't impose upon the patient and although tempted to pray, they should not spontaneously begin praying for the terminally ill without permission or a request. It may be that the terminally ill patient does not want prayer, does not believe in prayer or would rather not be bothered. In other words the chaplain should not assume or prejudge the patient. One can only do what the patient gives permission to do. Anything done without the patient's will is a violation of the patient's last moments and considered to be most devastating. The goal for the terminally ill patient is to make their last hours or last moments comfortable.

"PRESENCE" exemplifies and demonstrates to the patient that he or she is not alone. The remnant of a patient's days should not be spent agonizing over transitioning alone. We are here because God is here and we are compelled to represent Him in this transition of life. We have not come to argue with the patient about their beliefs or disbeliefs and yet, we are still charged to represent "faith" in God. We have either asked for permission or we have been requested to visit the patient. The patient should not have to argue their beliefs or disbeliefs at this time. The patient needs strength for each day's occurrences and challenges. We cannot forget that our primary focus is to offer an opportunity of peace, calm and acceptance for the present reality. Therefore we may have to comfort with great sensitivity and meet head-on that which is inevitable.

The "how" component involves availability and sensitivity to the concerns of the patient. We are concerned if the patient can hear, feel and express what they are feeling. We can check any preconceived notions or convenience at the door. These notions may encompass thoughts such as *I'll speak a few words of encouragement and uplift, I'll read a few of my favorite passages from the Bible, I'll end the encounter with a prayer and the sharing should not take more that fifteen minutes.* This type of behavior and thinking is inappropriate and more importantly, ineffective. The caregiver is devoted rather than duty driven and such behavior should never be exhibited in the presence of the patience. While the patient may not be able to articulate with precision what he or she is feeling and experiencing, the disposition of the caregiver should be patient and sensitive rather than frustrated. We are here to serve the patient. We must be willing of our own accord to make ourselves accommodating and available. Whatever the patient desires should be paramount to us as we journey to build their faith and acceptance.

Although we are committed and responsibly available, we also must encourage the patient to be open with us. It is a shared commitment and in many ways a relationship between patient and helper and it is important that the relationship is a good one. Some of the rigors and difficulties we encounter at first appear as a testing to determine the level of our commitment. The patient may have already experienced the loss of those who quit when the going got difficult. So they may put their worst out there first. After all they don't have the time to waste on an uncommitted relationship. Our level of commitment must be to uphold and hold up. We must be available, durable and usable to the patient, the family and friends. In this commitment to genuinely support the terminally ill, everyone is involved because it takes a team to win. Even the medical professionals are watching to see if we are making any difference or improvements in the patient's attitude, comfort and encouragement.

This brings us to the "why" component. Why are you here? The patient will have to release fears, frustrations, even anger that may be pent up inside to become prepared for the transition of life. Some of these issues are of long standing and have their own pain triggers. The patient's time clock will indicate the level of receptiveness for support. After the patient's testing has been completed and they begin reaching out to share quiet moments and thoughts, this is a good indicator that the patient has allowed the caregiver to step into their world. To get to the prize, we often have to pas the test. The patient has a need, to fully answer the "what" question. The patient in seeking to fulfill this need becomes ready and available to the support available. We don't want to miss our opportunity by being unavailable, nor do we want to be overaggressive and impatient. Wisdom is still the principal tool. We should continually pray for wisdom from God who gives men liberally. This is what they need to accomplish His will.

We speak many words in a day; some studies indicate we speak about 16 thousand words a day. With all these spoken words, do we understand the power and importance of the words we speak? Even idle words spoken have an effect on those who hear. Some words are life changing and once spoken cannot be rescinded. Some are powerful in application and definition and when properly understood enhance life. What you say and how you say it is important to the terminally ill. No voice or sound in the world is without meaning or without impact. When we consider our words, we are careful and deliberate in what we say. It is not in the multiplicity of words we speak but the genuineness of truth and love we express in our words. As persons chosen and selected, we are determined to complete the assignment with excellence to the terminally ill.

One powerful word is the word *prevail*. Simply defined, "to prevail" infers triumph; to persist, to become effective or effectual, being constant in action and opinions. To prevail includes having fortitude and determination. To prevail demonstrates an act of resistance against the enemy or foe, or to become victorious. A prevailing opinion is a dominant opinion or the most common exhibit, translation of action or activity in any given area. When we prevail we become consistent, amorous and victorious. To that end, our patient is prevailing in spite of the illness and disease which has come against them to steal, kill and destroy. The prognosis is, *this illness is terminal and will continue until death.* However, this does not mean that the enemy has prevailed, because death is not a victory over us or in us. The patient will die at some time or another just as we all will. However, death does not have the last word or the dominion.

The support we make available for the terminally ill has a purpose to make the continued life transition easier for the patient. The patient wants assurance that someone will be close and will care for them when death comes. The patient wants to be prepared with a sense of hope and victory. Sometimes patients are alone and without family or friend. Our "presence" becomes the surrogate family. Through careful listening we can recount important places in their lives. As the patient determines and navigates to meet death with dignity and victory, we are the troops marching alongside them. We hold up the banners of life to celebrate another hero going into transition. I have witnessed the last days or hours being the most coherent days of the patient's illness. They seem often to awake and become so alert asking for specific foods or items which seem unusual for their condition. I have seen the very last days being some of the best days during the illness.

Supporting and walking with the terminally ill models availability, which can further be explained by saying we strive to support the patient in their last moments of life. Our role in being available to the patient and their family is to have the listening ear for the concerns and complaints of the patient and the patient's family. The patient can trust us with the hearing and the interpretation of the words. Often fear, frustration and anger due to the loss of control engulfs them. The patient is dependent upon our listening ear to fully hear their concerns and to respond when they cannot. By this time the patient has been planted and watered sufficiently and now provided increase and reassurance in their final hours. We have ministered patiently in word, work and prayer so that the seed in them is ready to yield. The increase, like the glory, belongs to God.

The patient may well be expressing concerns that have festered over a lifetime. If we are honest, we all have areas and times when we have not understood the working of God. We must hear the complaints without correction or interruptions, allowing them to pour out of what has been filling and spilling, so we can pour back into them. Often before we can pour anything in we have to allow the patient to empty out. This is where our fruit of faith and patience comes in. We pray, not only believing God is hearing, but that He is also responding to helping us help the patient. This is the critical moment when the caregiver is called to share words of surety and calm assurance with the patient. We speak confidently and assuredly of the power, peace and effectualness of our God, who some call and identify as a higher power. Much of our time listening and being present has brought us to this very point. This is the moment where doubt, fear and death are swallowed up in victory. This is the time where God unfurls His banner of victory and we must be available, present and alert, listening carefully for this moment or we will miss the hero's parade.

"Presence" is helping the patient get beyond the "why" question; helping them to get beyond the pain and suffering is quite real. Yet with the presence of God, it is possible to go beyond. I know we thought once the patient was in acceptance that the "why me" was already done. Usually it will arise again as the illness becomes more pronounced and deeply seated. The "why" also helps the patient to envision and anticipate a place, according to the Word of God, which is far better than the best we could ever imagine. The "why" helps the patient to accept the future as whatever God wills and it releases their condition to God's sufficiency. We are sharing and helping the patient to understand that death is not their end. Life eternal has no end. One must learn to face death in the reality surrounding death. True acceptance is the cornerstone in assisting the terminally ill patient to move beyond their fear and doubts into faith.

Acceptance helps the terminally ill patient to experience their physical pain and hurt while knowing that this is a passing moment, a stop light on the road, a transition of life beyond what they have known. This knowledge is assuring and allows the patient to cry out for more acceptances in their understanding of their transition. We have awaited this cry with great anticipation; rejoice with the patient and things are well. The patient has endured hardship and trials and has emerged as a victor over the dark domain of death because their victory is already secured. The terminally ill person can now celebrate, even in the finality of this life, knowing that eternal life awaits them.

Terminal illnesses are not welcomed or easily explained, but they appear to be a part of life for reasons unknown to us. The secret things still belong to God and what belongs to us is only what is revealed according to His will. God has allowed illness to enter our world, not to defeat us although they do challenge us. Terminal illness is hard for many to accept because death is not accepted and understood by many as a transition. In a strange manner, God has allowed this woe with all its perplexities to aid us in our crying out to Him. Our patient is heard in the 90th Psalm, crying out to God as one being taught to *number their days and apply the heart to wisdom*. These events further certify our understanding that this form of life is temporal, short and simply a vapor that appears for a moment and then it is gone. From the dust we were made and to the dust we shall return. And still with all we don't understand, all things continue to work together for good for those who love God and are the called according to His purpose.

"Presence" affirms and reaffirms the truth of God that is in Christ and that life is the light of men. His life in us overcomes darkness, including the darkness we call death. The victory crown sits firmly upon the Head of the church and the believer. We celebrate today and participate in life eternally because of the work He has already done. The work of "Presence" brings faithful assurance to the bedside, transforming the sick room into a place where the wicked cease from troubling and the weary can rest in confidence.

Rest comes after the victory, after the battle has been won. It is the place where the fragrance of freedom and salvation fill the room. The peace of God takes the helm and victory is the name of the vessel we ride in, the great transition of life into greater life.

The transforming of the mind
opens the doors for healing
in accepting the diagnosis,
prognosis and moving into a
deeper relationship and
understanding of God.

Chapter 10

ACCEPTANCE—THE DOOR
OF ESCAPE

*T*he prison of our mind can be as entrapping as the prison of our physical being. Trapped, limited, powerless and without choices describes the cell with its door open to the incarcerated mind of the terminally ill. This entrapment is what they experience in their daily adjustment to the sentence of impending death. The lack of control in the small areas of life and the continual creeping in of what appears as the dominance of the illness, is like the coming nightfall experienced at the close of the day without the sunset. As in *The Never Ending Story*, the place called "Fantasia" is being overcome by "The Great Nothing." Desperation and futility are words lived as the human response to terminal illness. After all, the patient is still composed of flesh and blood, veins and arteries and as they begin to break down, the patient may also experience a breakdown of will and hope.

The atmosphere and surroundings of the terminally ill is vital. What we cannot change medically we can improve upon atmospherically and environmentally. When possible, it is vital to the terminally ill patient to get dressed and move outside the sick room to ease the feelings of entrapment and helplessness. We don't force one who cannot sustain themselves outside the bed to attempt a challenge beyond their abilities, however we encourage ambulatory patients to move outside. They may need to experience taking off the prison garb and moving beyond the cell of sickness that seems to trap and confine them. Little changes and splashes of color bring life into a sick room. We are not their cellmate or guard, but we are committed to bring liberty and light into a dismal and declining situation. Often the patient feels as though they are literally on death row doing a countdown of time until the execution. Goals in life have changed from plans or accomplishments to just making it pass the expected date of death. Faith has become an opportunity or a governor's reprieve as they search their lives for the offense that warranted this death sentence.

The picture of the big cat pacing in the small cell at the zoo is what they may feel like and we may appear as spectators. Regardless of the Bible reading, patients still have human responses of fear and anxiety. We are all are limited in what we can do because we are housed in an earthen and fragile body. Our human characteristics will continue to plague us even when we have accepted the illness and the diagnosis. The fight of faith is real and we must avoid casualties among those who are already terminally ill. Everyone wants a miracle. There isn't any reasonable explanation for the inoperable cancer, Alzheimer's or AIDS diagnosis that is destroying life. The diagnosis is as a ton of bricks on top of a helpless trapped body; it is heavier than can be endured. The prognosis is not laced with hope, so the feelings of victimization and incarceration are a daily contention. Our loved one is not living in a state of self pity; they are doing the best they can to live with a death sentence with no reprieve in sight.

The diagnosis and prognosis seem to have shut the door of escape. Our patient desires the door of escape to spring open. They may not have the strength to endure the illness to its end. To live everyday with the knowledge that your escape hatch is locked closed and you don't have the strength to open it is a self-condemning thought. To live without recourse, without a key and without relief or help can cause the one to experience feelings of isolation and imprisonment. The question of *where is God when I need Him* is very real to the patient. The fear of being conscious and living life to the end is dismal. The patient dreads the loss of independence caused by the illness. The pain, agony and futility they daily experience do not foster a victory song or a continual praise.

There are levels or degrees of acceptance and we want to help the patient negotiate through them and avoid the pitfalls of acceptance that may lead them headlong into hopelessness and self-destruction. Futility says, "Why even try, why even get up if death is the only option and is rapidly approaching? Why fight a battle you are not expected to win? Why use up your strength to fight one more day of the inevitable?" That is not the level of acceptance that is spiritually conducive to helping the terminally ill live in faith and not fear. This type of acceptance will not allow the patient to avoid becoming terminal in their spirit. A terminal spirit will embrace death as a welcomed friend. The flesh is sick and may be dying, but it is the spirit that is renewed day by day. The body is temporal but the spirit is eternal. The illness is terminal but the patient in faith is eternal. We can't overlook the humanity of the patient, the flesh and blood responses.

One of Aesop's fables is the story of "The Slave and the Lion." It is a simple story of the gratitude of a slave who, escaping from the cruelty of his master, sought refuge in an empty cave. The cave however was occupied, unknown to him, by a lion with a thorn in his foot. Instead of eating the slave the lion whined because of his injury. Being of a kindly heart, the slave removed the thorn and bandaged the wounds. For some time the slave and the lion lived together until the day the slave, desiring companionship of other humans, left the cave. He was soon captured and sent to the arena by the governor for execution. On the day of execution, he was put into the arena with the lions. One great roaring and furious lion rushed to him; but quietly laid at his feet was his friend, the lion from the cave. The governor, impressed by the act of friendship between the man and beast, set both of them free. Often the terminally ill want to enjoy this type of story ending. At some point we all want to believe the moral of the story should also apply to us and we can come to a truce with our adversary. If we have lived and have treated others with kindness, then the lions of life that confront us should simply lay down at our feet. However we find that this is not the penetrating reality of life when thrown in the arena of terminal illness.

Often the public and popular ministries encourage us to believe nothing bad will ever happen to good people. Somehow we are exempt from the cares and concerns that affect everyone else. We have no need of umbrellas, because even if it rains we won't get wet. It is contradictory in our minds to believe the same God who formed light also created darkness and He who makes peace, also created evil (*Isaiah 45:7*). We are unable to reconcile in ourselves the fact that God who is good can and does allow tragedies in the lives of His people. When these perplexities and tragedies come, we need the assurance that nevertheless, God remains with us and will keep us. At this point in our relationship with God, faith can afford us the peace, the comfort and the understanding that is needed. A relationship with God will not make everything alright overnight, but a genuine relationship gives us hope and strength when experiencing these difficult moments and trials of sickness and impending death.

Having a relationship with God will cause one to reach a spiritual level in knowing that suffering is a part of the natural life, a part of humanity. The moment of death is an appointment every man has which must be kept. God doesn't violate natural laws and we must accept the permissive will of God. One must accept whatever God wills. Though we act against God's will and God's plans, He never lets us down. He loves us deeply and completely. God has made an arrangement or an allowance and it is His permissive will. Though man has pulled away by selfishness selecting a way contrary to the best plans that God set for us, God never gives up on us. God allows His permissive will to be active in His people often in spite of our actions. Many times, we only fulfill His permissive will and refuse to fulfill His perfect will. Even when we decide to do what appears right to us, He loves and never deserts us. His love is the only reason for our not being forsaken and cast off. Only when we fulfill His perfect will can we receive His fullness of blessings.

The questions are often raised. Does God bring hardship on us? Do we bring hardship upon ourselves? Does faith attract adversity? Without getting into a lengthy discussion, everything God made is good and man in his complexity and disobedience implemented changes. Although God may not agree with man, He allows man to work against His will often to find his way to His will. How often have we learned lasting lessons by trial and failed methods? Simply speaking, consequences are a part of life. Man has often trampled over the very best that God has offered and has polluted God's blessings. Rather than eating at the Master's table, mankind has opted to eat from the feeding trough. This pollution has affected and infected mankind as a whole. Yet even in man's misappropriation of God's blessings, He is still forgiving and merciful towards humanity. God is still very capable of overlooking one's faults to meet their needs. Remember even when we are without faith, God is full of faith, for He cannot deny himself in us.

The patient who is without a God relationship will find this time most unbearable, disturbing, traumatizing and the future will appear hopeless. Depression and anger will begin to consume the body of the patient with more aggression than the illness. "Presence" is the 911 call to get them to faith as quickly as possible. Helping the patient to find hope in the midst of suffering is our challenge. Without this hope the impossibilities for life will overcome the terminally ill. "Presence" helps the patient find hope and the will to cooperate with the help available. This is neither an easy journey, nor a simplistic resolve to all the cares of our terminally ill, family members or friends, but it is where we start.

When the terminally ill patient lives in acceptance of the illness, the healing process can begin. This process includes both a physical and a mental healing. **The transforming of the mind opens the doors for healing in accepting the diagnosis, prognosis and moving into a deeper relationship and understanding of God.** Faith gives needed help and the beginning of experiencing inner healing for the terminally ill. The mind is no longer a prisoner at the physical level. The jail door really can spring open at this faith level because faith in God is able to do exceedingly and abundantly beyond and above our expectation according to His power working in us. Did we really think the jail doors for Paul and Silas opened because of a song? No, it was because of the undoubting faith that would not submit to fear or failure. Faith opens the door for the power of God to become active in us. Faith releases us from the power of sickness and into the liberty of God. Faith is the first step in the journey to freedom.

As previously indicated, when the terminally ill patient rejects the illness, they will experience different stages of grief. Without acceptance the impact of the facts of the illness will overwhelm and incapacitate the patient. Denial and rejection of facts hinder faith from working; it is a stop light. We cannot apply faith where denial and rage reside. When refusing to accept the results of medical testing, the patient becomes angry with everybody and anybody. The nucleus of the anger, many times, is the illness itself or the means by which the disease was contracted. The anger becomes as acid eating away at the patient. Their ability to resist is weakened. The focus or direction of the anger is really towards God. It is often verbalized as, "if God is," or "if God can," or "if not now, then when is the time for miracles?" "Why don't I deserve to be the woman with the issue of blood or the man born blind? Why can't I be Lazareth who is called back to life as a testimony to the greatness of God? Why punish me and let criminals continue to live?"

The rhetorical questions continue: "God why? Why did you let this terrible thing happen to me?" It is God who is exposed to and the target of the disbelief and anger of man. But God remains gracious, forgiving and merciful. The patient who rejects reality is depressed and closed to the intervention of God. A patient, with no hope, no smile, no laughter is just a fading flower void of fragrance. The patient can no longer find joy in life because bitterness and remorse are devouring whatever life they have left. The patient has allowed the illness to overwhelm their spirit, mind and body becoming victorious over the quality of life they have left. The patient can be a picture of brokenness, hopelessness, full of sorrow and self pity, unable to receive the renewal God can provide in the most adverse conditions. As a child, I would marvel at the bus driver who sat behind a wheel and made an even bigger bus turn sharply. God does that all the time. He has in His hand the big wheel that turns the situations of life around. He only asks us to believe.

It is one thing to be locked in the prison by the guard who walks the hall with the clanging keys. It is another thing to lock yourself up behind the bars with rejection and rage. When the patient refuses to realistically deal with the reality of their situation, the prison door is shut tight and they are holding the keys. The key to faith is first understanding and believing that the condition exists, but nothing is too great for God. Accepting the illness as fact and the truth that physicians have exhausted their abilities opens up our spirit, mind and body for the intervention of something greater than humanity. Faith doesn't work void of the acknowledgement of the existence of a condition or circumstance requiring its work. Faith in the life of the terminally ill is an active ingredient and not a passive emotion. We cannot expect God to work where nothing exists or to work in a vacuum. Faith is the key unlocking the door of possibilities in us. In rejection of the facts, the patient can waste precious time trying to locate a physician to confirm a hope while allowing the illness to advance.

Faith motivates and doesn't stagnate. With faith, the patient is able to move beyond medical facts and chooses to live every moment of life fully. They have chosen not to drown in self pity or remorse where grief becomes larger than life and where they simply give up and surrender to death. Faith helps the patient not to isolate himself from everything and everybody or crawl into a shell and wait for death to come. Without faith, the patient has predetermined their end and may cease to eat, communicate or refuse to take medicines. This can help enhance the progression of the illness, affording them less time with family and loved ones. It also deprives them of the time for additional resistances to be built up in their bodies. A message of hope sends a clear message of victory to the illness; "you have invaded my body but you have not destroyed my spirit." Without hope, God cannot or will not, heal me. You fall into a state of, "Let me die because I choose death rather than this life of hopelessness."

A lack of faith tragically results in the loss of the desire to fight and the loss of the desire to live. By refusing to remain positive or optimistic, the patient yields to death. In many cases the patient can become suicidal in their loss of faith and they decide to terminate life, which is both tragic and unchristian. Since we did not give life, it is not ours to take from ourselves. Whatever the cost, we must cling to our faith, not allowing sickness or even death to unhinge us and steal life from us. God is our refuge and strength, a present help in every situation. In Hebrews 11:39, faith heroes are commended for their perseverance, even if it didn't bring the results they wanted. Faith is a victory in the midst of our crisis. Regardless of the grim medical facts, the dismal prognosis and events evidenced in our physical bodies, faith still makes us unashamed and victorious. We must always believe God above the circumstances and evidences to the contrary. Faith is being assured in knowing there is hope available when things are not looking good and every day the news continues to increase at a rate that overwhelms us.

Often we are taught to deny the existence of illness or disease as a testament to our faith. However to accept terminal illness rather than reject it is a positive. This type of positive thinking keeps us open to help and support while traveling along this road of terminal illness. Every day that the patient is alive is a milestone and an active victory over the illness. Miracles are still a work of God in today's society. Although the patient may not invest all their energy and efforts in seeking the possibility of a miraculous healing, I would encourage you to practice applying faith in healing. Biblically speaking, God is seen and witnessed as a healer. To remove His ability to heal from the equation is simple foolishness. Biblical documentation depicts many who were healed of terminal illnesses. Some included Simon's mother-in-law who was sick of fever. The captain named Naaman had leprosy. These are just a few who experienced God's intervention in their situation and were healed. The basis of miracles is faith. Often medical professionals are astounded by remissions, improvements, extensions of life and they have no medical explanation.

Acceptance is only the first step towards the healing of the mind. *Resignation* is the belief that something as inescapable, unchangeable and surrendering or submitting your future to it. You have given in, handing over your individual power to another power. When applied to terminal illness this means forfeiting days of joy and companionship for days of despair and welcoming the darkness. You cannot experience the joy or peace of God and you miss recalling precious memories and the companionship of family and friends because you are committed to dying. You now allow the bed you may be confined to, to become your jail. You fail to enjoy laughter or the lighter moments of living while living. Resignation leaves void of pleasures; this is not acceptance. Resignation is a mindset that closes the mind to intervention.

"Presence" helps the patient strive to live, to look beyond their present sufferings, pain and frustrations, which are very real. Yesterday becomes the honey in the bitter tea of today with help and reassurance. Effective ministry is there to help the terminally ill patient reach into the treasure chest that God has filled with pleasant and wonderful moments for them to hold and to cherish. Some terminally ill patients have lived hard and exhausting lives. Recalling the fortitude needed to get through the past can help the patient summon the strength and faith to live fully today. They have always been warriors and now they can call upon the warrior in them to help them gain and push back the intruder. The treasure chest is full of valuable helps to brace the terminally ill for the hardness of today. They now need to let faith arise.

We who decided to give genuine support to the terminally ill must always be aware of our humanity. We cannot continue to scream religious truths as an echo without understanding the realities of the terminally ill patient. We are not here to judge or interpret how they should respond or testify as to how we would respond if it were us. The fact is, this is the mountain they must climb and the river they must cross. We are helpers of our brothers and sisters, the hands that reach across the aisles and across the hospital bed. Represent consistent and steady help with understanding in their time of crisis. We are human and as such, we comfort. We are a companion and stimulation to our loved ones in the hours of weakness, confusion and dismay. We continue to represent His presence in the lives of the terminally ill and share the faith and the testimony of His faithfulness. In a moment when He can't be seen or felt, He is actively working through and in us to reassure and comfort the weak and desolate of heart.

We cannot be the occasional visitor. We are called to be the constant friend who sticks by in the hour of adversity. The terminal illness is adversity; it is aggressive and seeks victory and we come to aid our comrade in the fight for life. "Presence" comes to the wounded and despondent with support and refreshment in the midst of the battle. We come not with all the answers but we must come with as much information as possible to understand the many situations the terminally ill face. We continue to demonstrate the faithfulness and concern of God, as we love the patient and their family, even on those days when they are less communicative than others — even on the days when the patient is aggressive or very vocal in their disappointment. In sharing with the terminally ill, we know our own humanity and therefore our patient's humanity. Our persistency is being tested and we brace ourselves, fueling ourselves in the word, in prayer and genuine fellowship. We are revived even in the presence of human pain and suffering to assist the terminally ill.

By understanding the process
we are prepared to help
in the warfare of the mind,
as thoughts of terminated life
invade and attempt to possess
the mind. We can help the patient
recall faith as the victory that
overcomes the world.

SECTION III: THE TERMINAL CHALLENGE

Chapter 11

FAITH CHALLENGES OUR HUMANITY

*O*n those days when Superman takes the day off and people are able to reflect on his humanity, faith in a super hero seems questionable. Humanity is a rival to our faith; it is who we are inwardly. Our human frame is weak in and of itself and without faith it will fail us. Although we are Spirit filled, we are housed in a human suit. The humanity of the terminally ill patient is in need of sincere support, well defined and not questioning or debating. We are not in conflict with the patient but a companion and help even in times of conflict. Often we must consider with understanding, that regardless of how impossible or irrational an action or reaction may be, it is still a human response to the intrusion of a predator, terminal illness. The "good" death is not something we have practiced or are prepared for unless we are in a theatrical production as an actor training for the big night. In real life we are not always afforded the opportunity to die the death we want without pain or emotions. We are not museum pieces frozen in time to satisfy the viewing audience, and the exit doors before us are not the way we desire to leave the building.

"Presence" is providing unconditional support where the humanity of our loved one is not only tolerated but sincerely understood. We amass information to make a deliberate and helpful response to the patient's daily changing situation. Every day the terminally ill patient awakes from an attempted sleep with the knowledge that the sand in the hourglass is spilling quickly from the top to the bottom. One can say that everyone is aware of the days of their lives passing ever so quickly. Yet at the announcement of the terminal illness, the sands begin to move more quickly than before. The patient becomes more aware of the days passing. Once the sand in the hourglass reaches midpoint, it begins to hasten to its end. We cannot expect the terminally ill to be detached or emotionless after the declaration of impending death. This announcement is a reversal of the birthday song. They cannot take a clinical look at death void of an emotional response or attachment or fondness to life. In the process of acceptance there must be room for self grieving. The patient is grieving the losses of memories not yet actualized and events that are on the horizon of hope and that may never be experienced or seen.

I have often thought a life worth living is also worth grieving over its loss or absence. The terminally ill patient, as well as their families who will be left behind, is grieving even in the midst of life. The truth is, life is precious and everyone wants his or her life to have been memorable and full. We all want to have accomplished some specific things that only we have put importance upon. They are our personal hallmark events and occasions to be enjoyed and remembered. We desire to celebrate successes and to sit back in our older years and remember the cost of them. The terminal illness not only puts those potential celebrations to death but also the prognosis and actuality of the decline of health that is presently in a debilitating state. The continual pain and loss of independence makes acceptance of the diagnosis a truth to the patient although it will never be accepted as a choice or an event that can be embraced. One can certainly want to go to heaven and yet not want to die. The grim reality has been accepted because it is truth; it is a fact and not the good news of life desired.

I am a musician and a lover of all kinds of music. I know the power of music to comfort, encourage and lift the spirits. I know its depths can touch the soul when words cannot. One wrong note can change the atmosphere in a recital hall or spoil a perfect movement in *Beethoven's Piano Sonata No. 28.* No matter how we practice to be perfect we can inadvertently hit that wrong note; we can become distracted by the loss of melody. However, even when we play or hear the wrong note we can't disregard the entire piece. So it is when humanity surfaces that we glimpse the strain, fear, anger and hopelessness. Life with its complications can cause us to want to disappear and to disengage. It is human. The terminally ill person can openly discuss, without shame, the feelings of fear and hopelessness that accompany the illness. We care and provide understanding, comfort and concern for what they are enduring.

In treating terminal illness, palliative care is used to soothe the symptoms without ever curing the disease itself. The inevitability of death is still not a welcoming attraction in our theater even when symptoms are eased. Regardless of the wonder and greatness of heaven our members opt for life and rightly so. The discussion of what to do keeps the reality of the terminal state of the illness before the patient. We should not be surprised that the thought of suicide begins to invade the conversation of the terminally ill. Humanly, whenever possible we all want to avoid the unpleasant and painful potholes of life. Many of us have experienced seeing a pothole in the road and swerving to avoid it rather than running the risk of damaging our vehicle, much to the dismay of the driver in the next lane beeping his horn. Therefore thoughts of ending it all, removing oneself from the struggle should not surprise us or annoy us. They are thoughts of swerving to miss the pothole looming just ahead of the patient. It is not what we approve; however we understand the desire to forego the events preceding the end.

We cannot be surprised if depression and thoughts of suicide begin to invade the conversations and become part of the expression of the frustration and hopelessness that the patient maybe experiencing. Suicidal thoughts begin at the point of acceptance of the prognosis of terminal illness. At that point our loved one has probably already discussed DNR [do not resuscitate] orders in the hospital. Hospice care may have already been presented or accepted once hospital care was no longer an option. Hospital care is curative and the illness is not considered curable. When the quality of life is lost, the patient can view living as worthless. They see themselves hanging on the sickroom wall for viewing or as a distorted reflection of what they once were, now for visiting or viewing. To hasten the inevitable may well appear as an acceptable option to an agonizing ending. Why not put an end to all the suffering of mental and physical agony? After all, that would be humane, wouldn't it? Many people in today's society agree that the painless, humane and reasonable response to terminal illness is euthanasia.

Euthanasia is defined by some as the answer to the excessive costs incurred with a terminal illness. The terminally patient may well see themselves as a financial burden upon their families. Medical treatment even if it is palliative care is still financially exhausting. Medical insurance coverage will only pay part of the expenses incurred. The patient may view themselves as an extravagance that their family simply cannot afford. They may consider in their absence that time and money could be saved. Why not consider the painless ending of life as a welcomed alternative to suffering? They may also consider the inability to help. Having to be waited on is an additional hindrance, an inconvenience for those they love and who love them. The loss of bodily functions or other distresses of the illness can and does have a psychological effect on the patient and their family.

To choose euthanasia is to leave God out of the process and to say, "God, the problem is bigger than you and bigger than me. I'll make it easier on both of us and end my life." In James 4:14 life is described as a vapor, a mist that appears for a very short period and then vanishes. Euthanasia is not a biblical practice. It is not the Christian perspective. God wants us to love life and preserve life to its very last moment. Life is precious and is to be valued. The limited use of our mind and feeble efforts of our brain cannot begin to embrace what God can and cannot do. God still challenges humanity to have the faith and believe that miracles can come forth. Regardless of man's inability, God supersedes him in ability. God's abundance is beyond man's reason. God can move, can heal, can restore and mend in unimaginable ways. Self destruction, euthanasia and suicide are the result of a critical, but human "faith shut down."

It is in the human condition of man to despair in adversity. In 1 Corinthians 1:8, Paul writes to the Corinthians regarding the trouble he and his companions endured while in Asia. He speaks of their being burdened beyond measure, above strength, despairing of life and having a death sentence within. Yet in the midst of this sentence of death they refused to be persuaded. They did not have faith or confidence in anything except God, who delivered them from a great death. This same word "persuaded" is used in Romans 8:38 when Paul says *he is persuaded, confident that nothing; not death, life, angels, principalities, powers present or to come have the ability to separate him for God's eternal love.* Terminal illness may have come, but God has not decreased life's value because of terminal illness and neither can we. The life of the terminally ill patient is of great value and our constant and continual presence is a reminder of that invaluableness.

Most people who are terminally ill become depressed because they suffer the loss of control in their lives, their bodies and future. As the terminally ill person demonstrates more aggressive feelings of hopelessness, their way of thinking, which can be negative, intensifies. One feels the overwhelming loss or the slipping away of control without any hope of regaining it. Much has been lost as the illness continues to escalate. The patient's view of the world has become small and distorted, sometimes only as big as the one room they spend much of their time in. The patient may be immobile or limited in their ability to leave the house. How do they control or dominate a world where sickness appears to rule? As these truths mount, they bring with them thoughts of putting an end to the illness, now rather than later. The physical pain of the illness is compounded by the physiological pain. Death seems to have the last word. The continual loss of control could be regained by choice to cheat death of its final victory. **By understanding the process we are prepared to help in the warfare of the mind, as thoughts of terminating life invade and attempt to possess the mind. We can help the patient recall faith as the victory that overcomes the world.**

Since death is already on the table and in the conversation of terminal illness, it may seem like only a small step, an alternative option from the illness to self destruction. In a world that struggles with the issues of life choices, a death choice is not a foreign or uncommon alternative. In a permissive society which gives credence to almost any responsive action with a voice of understanding, we must speak clearly and compassionately of the value of life. Remaining connected to the terminally ill continually affirms the value God has put on life. Since the day the doctor gave the patient the diagnosis of terminal illness, the thoughts of death and dying have been a part of the daily internal and external conversations. The patient has been saying silent good-byes and preparing for death. Deliberate and prepared ministry carefully and caringly continues to build faith in the midst of the inner turmoil the patient and their family are experiencing.

Often the families of the patient are pressured to forgo treatments because they are too expensive, pointless and draining on them. They are experiencing the guilt of making choices that seem to be giving up on the life of their loved ones. The weight is upon them to make what are life and death decisions. The thief has come robbing them of the ability to be at peace with their responses to the illness. The patient, seeing the strain, would like at this point to alleviate it by leaving this world with some dignity and not being helpless or infantile. Often they will express the thoughts that their families would be better off without them or they are concerned the insurance they have left will be swallowed up by excessive medical expenses. They may well begin to encourage or request their family members to turn off or stop any treatment and let them die. This is an emotionally draining and discouraging time for the patient and their family.

The humanity of man in his desire to forego suffering and ease his death is not new. In 1 Samuel 31:3-6 King Saul was severely or terminally wounded. He had lost his sons, was losing the battle and his entire kingdom.

This king pleads with his armor bearer to kill him, to put him out of his misery. His humanity cried out to put an end to his suffering, humiliation and pain before his enemies triumphed over him. Since his servant would not do it, he took his sword and fell upon it and took his own life. There may have been many good reasons for King Saul to do what he did, just as it may seem reasonable to the terminally ill; however it is not God's will that man would take his own life, to fall upon his sword hopeless. A prepared ministry to the terminally ill understands, but it does not support or encourage this action; we can minister to the terminally ill without theological debates and arguments. It is the simple reminder that men do not belong to themselves; they are secured with a price — the price God paid for them in love. He is the giver of life.

The reminder of the love of God, which can transform any life situation and attitude, is why we have faith in Him. With faith in God's word, death becomes a comma rather than a period. Death becomes that transition into a better life, a grander existence. The Bible declares, "Eyes have not seen and ears have not heard, neither have entered into the heart of man, the things which God hath prepared for them that love him." We believe death doesn't separate us from God's love; it is that transition chamber to the other side of eternal peace from our side of imperfections, darkness, brokenness, destruction, pain, suffering, disappointments and self hatred. We will one day experience His presence, which is a refuge from the ills and trials of this world, an eternal peace and a sense of completion and wholeness in which there is no end.

When these thoughts begin to control the thinking of the patient, it is a good time to make a change. If the patient is ambulatory, it may be a good time to go outside or bring something different into their environment. It can be something ever so simple: music, a beautiful scarf for thinning hair, a body spray or lotion, a picture book or a plant. It is the simple things that remind people of their value. Perhaps you can plan to visit on a day or evening when the family has something to do and give them a clear mind about missing their visit. It can be a time when both the patient and the primary caregiver need a rest. Often the patient is unable to attend church and a DVD of the service or listening to the CD can provide fellowship. Allowing the caregiver to go to service while you and the patient spend a morning together can be refreshing for both. The ministry of "Presence" continues to utilize every opportunity to demonstrate the love and care God has in the fundamental support we can provide.

The ministry allows the entire church the opportunity to become involved in the support of the terminally ill. In these times of contradictions of thoughts, it may be a time to encourage our youth department to make a thoughtful card. Our missionaries may send cards to remind the patient that they are important and that they represent the rooting of the home team. The ministry keeps the pastor and staff current on the condition of the patient and their family. Often deacons or associate ministers will visit as an encouragement. It is the small almost seemingly everyday kindness that makes the difference in the life of the terminally ill patient. When the church is involved with the ministry, the patient can experience the true fellowship of the saints and the value of life is validated. The membership is staying connected by receiving updates in the corporate and intercessory prayer groups, and all of these activities serve as a reminder to the patient and their family that they are important to God and others.

There are many conversations we can have to remind the terminally ill person they are often and fondly remembered. We continue to represent God and the body of Christ in all we do. We are delegated by God and trained by our pastors to effectively and knowledgeably minister to the spiritual and emotional needs of the patient and their family. We are helpers of one another, a present help in the time of need. Blessing them truly blesses us.

It is not wrong or unchristian to want to avoid pain and suffering. After all, we don't rush to the edge of the cliff in order to jump off, but we go there to enjoy the view.

Chapter 12

FAITH—THE CHALLENGE
TO FUTILITY

*G*od is rich in His benefits to us as we review the treasure filled boxes in us holding our wonderful memories to revisit and to cherish. They are the photo albums of the heart to be opened in times of great distress. These wonderful memories are often tucked away in the secret and hidden places of our lives. We visit them in times of loneliness, distress or when we are overwhelmed and disappointed. They validate our lives. They are the birthday celebrations, anniversaries and the turkey eating holidays, family reunions, graduations and comforts locked away in the secure storage bins of the heart. As Barbara Streisand once sang, *"Memories, Like the corners of my mind, misty water-colored memories, of the way we were. Scattered pictures, of the smiles we left behind, smiles we gave to one another for the way we were...."* These memories may be few, but all of us have some. Even when life has been challenging, we have our individual treasure chest of memories to get us through.

Life is full of twists, turns and events that can cause abrupt and challenging changes in our journey, holding us hostage at one life check point or another. Often when I have been traveling abroad, I am stopped at customs to verify that I am who I represent myself to be. I have to pull out the passport and show documentation of my identity. I have learned to keep the passport in a convenient and secure place where it can be quickly displayed. The passport not only contains my snapshot but also the history of my journeys. It gives credence to my right to be there and to continue traveling. In a very real way the passport not only identifies me, it also validates who I am and the place of my home citizenship. When traveling, you are cautioned to protect your passport and to keep it secure because there are thieves who would steal your identity. They would leave you lost, abandoned and wandering in a strange place without any means of identification. John 10:10 says it is the thief who comes to steal, kill and destroy; but God comes to enlarge and abundantly fill our lives.

As the passport is necessary, so are the memory passports of days and smiles of our past. They are helpful medicine to the soul and body as you travel along this road of terminal illness. You may be restricted to the bed and the body may be too weak to support itself, but your memories can be your passport, your strong anchor, reminding you of your identity and validating your right to be where you are. These memories of joy, accomplishments and inclusion support terminally ill patients when facing these last days. The patient's recall of yesterday's laughter, fellowships and friendships with loved ones are supports to their overall well being. The memories of mistakes can also be beneficial in giving the patient time to repent, reconcile and time to renew relationships. This makes tomorrow necessary as another day to enjoy a renewed relationship.

Well being are still words that can be used for the terminally ill as the sense of purpose and belonging. We are there to share and relive the memories, storing them as medicinal injections for the patient. Hope and revival memories have a wonderful way of transforming the condition, lightening the darkness and transporting the patient into a happier, healthier, stronger and calmer place. They refresh and are a source of bringing pleasure and relief. Often even the rehearsal of losses can assist in giving the terminally ill patient a reason to continue to live as they are a reminder of the mountains they have already climbed over in life. Tomorrow is another day to repay, revive and heal those less than perfect relationships.

In the process of accepting an illness as terminal there is the need to also accept the power, mercy, love and eternality of God. One must believe that God is in control even when pain and death are imminent. Our days are numbered and God has not forgotten nor forsaken us in the mathematics of life. We remain the treasury of God and He holds His treasure in our earthen vessels. The vessel may be earthen and tempo-ral but the contents are eternal and precious. We are His chosen people and as the Apostle Paul reminded us in Romans 8:28, *all things collaborate as good for those who love the Lord and who are the called according to His purpose.*

Over the centuries we have understood this passage to include sickness, despair, brokenness, unemploy-ment, darkness, disappointment, death, divorce, deser-tion and even separation from our children. Men and women have comforted themselves in war, famine, earthquakes and every adversity and challenge of life knowing it is included in the *"all things that work to-gether."* The list of infinite, individualized and indefin-able events included in our human experience are included in the *"all things."* Faith knows, whatever hap-pens in life, the good, the bad and the unexpected, hap-pens to us all and is for our good and His glory. No, they don't appear as all good or even feel good, but faith trusts God in the outcome. This is hard to accept when the thing happening seems to extinguish the candle of our life. The strength of one's faith and relationship with God is an important factor in the acceptance of the "good" that can come from one's terminal illness or ter-minal situation.

The impossibility of facing a terminal illness void of faith in God is to live life without the assurance of God being with and in you throughout life's journey. Remind the terminally ill patient that life's passport, having been already validated, is an essential part in knowing that they can endure to the end. It is not enough for us to stand on this sideline of life holding the patient's hand, being cordially present in this temporal existence and not prepare them for things to come in the final chapter of life. As genuine care givers, we reinforce and reload faith which may become drawn and weakened by the daily fight for life. It is necessary to provide consistent and genuine "presence" to the terminally ill during this personal and draining crisis. Helping the patient to acknowledge, restore and maintain faith keeps their God connection intact. Don't forget that the terminally ill patient is still on the journey of life; God is still present and His Holy Spirit as their guide. We continue to stoke the faith embers of the heart, breaking open to release the fire stored in them and reminding them of the daily or even moment by moment power of the presence of God. We keep faith in God alive in the patient helping them access its unquenchable fire in their hours of need.

Even when one cannot physically walk we are commanded to walk despite our conditions *by faith and not by sight.* Walking by faith has nothing to do with being whole or standing erect. We are to walk not by what is evident but by what we believe and trust from within, to affect us outwardly. This is often seen clearly when we continue to press on in spite of the obstacles and land-mines in our path. Death may well be eminent and looming before the terminally ill and still, faith is the in-tangible pillar of strength, hope and determination that allows one to walk by faith even when lying flat on their back. All the heroes of the day are not those who are seen on the white horses or marching with their limbs intact into the battle. Many heroes have held the line of battle wounded and weakened but they hold on regard-less of the pain. Victory is not always seen. It is more often the unseen heroes who receive their honors by the Commander in Chief. A strong presence is faith in ac-tion and it continually conveys, encourages and gives support even in this hard hour of what appears as the final testing and acceptance.

The terminally ill need a strong representation and articulation of the eternal matters of life, which are quickly approaching. All of us naturally want to avoid suffering and we do not welcome pain. We are not at the airport flagging in the pain and discomfort as a wel-comed transport. Our humanness doesn't seek the pain or loss of life as our greatest reward. **It is not wrong or unchristian to want to avoid pain and suffering. After all, we don't rush to the edge of the cliff in order to jump off, but we go there to enjoy the view.** There is a survival network in us all. We do all we can

to preserve our lives and extend them. Our brain man-
ufactures agents of relief called endorphins. They are
natural pain relievers acting as sedatives to suppress
pain. These are the body's self-preservation agents that
help us endure and overcome. When we see danger, we
maneuver to find a place of safety to bypass those dangerous obstacles. Even when riding bicycles or climbing
mountains, we wear head gear to protect us from injury.
We are not pain seekers and yet when pain, illness and
discomfort come, we need our faith to get us through it
and help us continue on the next leg of our journey. Our
faith is as medicinal as any medicine or human agency
of healing.

The working together for good by all things in life that
Paul speaks of cannot be detected or seen in the moments of enduring pain that seem unbearable and continual. Often the pain will block our hope and
disappointment and fatigue will distort our view and
perception. Paul encourages and compels believers to
continue in faith and accept whatever comes to be
within the scope of God's will and in His control. Everything will not be easily understood by us in its inception.
Life is full of questionable events, but faith puts the en-
tirety of the matter into God's hands when reason is
nullified. C. A. Tindley, one of the great hymn writers,
musicians and composers penned a hymn entitled, *We'll
Understand it Better By and By.* It reads like this:

We are often tossed and driven on the restless sea of time.
Somber skies and howling tempests often precede a bright sunshine.
In that land of perfect day, when the mist have rolled away,
We'll understand it better, by and by.
By and by, when the morning comes,
When the said of God gather home,
We'll tell the story, how we've overcome...
For we'll understand it better, by and by.

Through poetry and music, he has given us insight into the concept that many times we do not understand. We cannot see the good in disappointment, terminal illness and the tragic events of life. Yet, when we are confident of the eternalness of life, we hold on, in faith, to what we cannot understand now. It is in that *land of perfect day,* when everything obscuring our perception, hindering our ability to see, *has rolled away* that we will understand what we now need faith to receive and live through. He reminds us that it is in the *by and by* or in the eternalness of the matter our understanding is enlightened and we will know Him, being like Him, as we are known of Him. Therefore we will understand it better by and by. In other words, we will overcome the bitterness of today in the sweetness of our tomorrow life. Discouragement comes. Pain is real and yet faith is just as real as the pain we feel.

To accept terminal illness is to accept a condition which is always subject to God's divine intervention. God's divine will embraces man's free will and braces him for the indeterminate or the not known in advance will and working of God. What we don't know can hurt us because we cannot tap into it to help us. Before we accept God's will, we must first receive His Lordship in our lives. It is impossible to accept His will if He hasn't been accepted in our hearts in His fullness. This acceptance allows us to be open and available for all blessings of healing and restoration of our physical body. When man, with his medical expertise in healing and curative powers, has reached his limit and exhausted his abilities, faith in God ushers us to a place of peace. Without faith in God, we have no hope of healing. We are held up at customs and cannot move forward. We must live whatever time is left in hope or confidence that only God has the conclusion to the matter of living.

The ministry is needed to help keep salvation and the open and continual confession and expression of God present in the room and heart of the terminally ill. We cannot close the door of faith in God in the acceptance of the diagnosis; but we put our prophetic foot in the door keeping it from closing. Paul states in Romans 5:5 that there is a hope that keeps us from shame, dishonor and defeat. We must not forget that God can prolong and restore life. He is life and His life became light within man through faith. Faith helps us, encouraging us not to trust physicians more than we trust God at work in us. I must reiterate the diagnosis of terminal illness stipulates that man has reached his limit of helping; this does not limit what God can or will do. When man has failed and cried, "Impossible," God moves in and does His best work. Our hope, belief and relief should not be in man but in God. Man's ability at its best is limited, while God's is without limits for he is boundless.

God can turn things around and He has a sure record of turning things around. In the Bible, Hezekiah's life was turned around when God added fifteen years to his life after he received the death sentence for the next morning. It may seem that God is not moving miraculously for us, but we must not count God out of the equation. Cancer patients, AIDS patients, Alzheimer's patients and many others have lived past their expected survival dates pushing their way through by faith. Even newborns not expected to live through the night have miraculously, not only lived through the night, but lived long lives. God has brought deliverance and healing in the midst of a terminal diagnosis and He has turned things around. Remember the woman with the *issue of blood*? After twelve years of being homebound, sick, rejected, destitute and hemorrhaging, she was healed and restored by the virtue present in the presence of Jesus. We cannot close the door on the miraculous working of God in us and for us because man is limited.

In accepting their illness and situation the terminally ill patient should also be open to God's ability to turn things around. The patient's understanding and commitment to God should stand, even if God chooses not to heal. God must remain, even when the terminally ill is disappointed, distressed and feeling disconnected from family; it is necessary for the patient to remain responsive to Him and trust Him.

This was the mindset of the Hebrew boys who were thrown into the fiery furnace for not bowing down before the King (*Daniel 3:19-25*). In the face of a fatal decision rendered by the King, they were convinced that God was able to deliver them. They were open to God's will, God's decision and had genuine faith in God's ability. The thought of losing their lives or keeping their lives was not a primary concern. The focus was the security in knowing that whatever happened they would be doing God's will. In doing God's will, they would be drawn closer to Him. To live or die, to experience another birthday or not, should not be the nucleus of a Christian's life. The focus should be to appreciate the NOW and the blessings of God which affords us peace, strength and understanding to embrace His will with confidence in

Him; this is the definition of joy.

The struggle of the terminally ill is to get beyond the NOW, the immediate pain and suffering and begin thanking God for that which has already happened, that which is in the NOW. It is not worrying endlessly about life or death. It is in the NOW moment that the grace of God can be experienced. To know that God's ultimate will and His power are not diminished by sickness, death or life is invigorating. Our goal should not be what we want God to do, but what God wills to do. It is living in the "nevertheless" of God. We never receive less from God even when we don't receive what we want or understand of His working. We learn to pray for the strength to remain steadfast in His love, unmovable by the circumstances and undefeated in our struggles. Our humanity may demand evidence from God for His faithfulness and assurance of His love by giving us the desire of our hearts. In Psalms 8:4, the psalmist acclaims the greatness and the enormity of God who is continually mindful of man. The conditions of man fill the mind of God always. God owes man nothing, but we owe Him everything.

We want the promises of long life and to live beyond the expected time and even more when we have walked in faith all our lives. We have honored our father and mother with the promise of our days being extended in the earth as a reward. We may well have lived exceptional lives of faith, giving ourselves to others and ministering to those who are oppressed and without. We have endured hardship and continued to fight the good fight of faith to now come to this place where we are suffering a daily dying. Often we desire God to operate in equity or fairness to us, especially when we have lived honorably. Without saying it, we want God to be as faithful to us as we see ourselves having been to Him. When our stockings are hung by the chimneys with care we hope to awake to the fullness of them. This terminal illness is like coal in our faith stockings. It is not the response we are expecting having lived a life of faith, yet in this moment, in one doctor's visit, life changed. But, regardless, our faith must remain intact. We cannot leave God now, although we are angry, hopeless and despondent.

The faith we have walked in all our lives is needed even more at the end of life. It is in the closing chapters of the book when the whole story comes into focus. There have been many events, trials, plots, moves and motives in the book of our lives. But, in the closing chapters, we can see the purpose of the events; the glory and essence of the faith of the faithful shines through. "Presence" is called into the room to polish the gold that has been tried by the fire. Gold can be found underwater. When being mined, it is panned and then sifted through mesh to separate the gold from the ordinary rocks. When it is encased in hard rock it can be separated from the casing surrounding it by picks, hammers or even chemicals such as cyanide. The purpose of mining is to extract the valuable gold from what has surrounded and encased it. Sometimes sickness is the encasing of the gold. We must see the faith inside the terminally ill patient and help them to live in the value of their faith all the days of their life, to see the glory of God released from the casing of doubt, hopelessness and fear that is a our human response.

We are not hammering away at the terminally ill patient as a relentless miner looking for the treasure hidden within them. However, knowing the keeper of the treasure is God and the treasure is held in our earthen vessel (*2 Corinthinas 4:7-11*), we can encourage the patient to revisit the faith they have always enjoyed or explore their recently-discovered faith. Genuine support helps the patient to receive and define the value of the excellence of God in them, to help and aid themselves in these final hours. Help is needed to reassure the patient that even in the final hours of life, in the struggle for life and in the presence of death, God is still alive in them. Because He lives, they will always live. Regardless of the outcome in the natural sense, death does not have dominion or authority over the life of the faithful. Their lives are in the hands of God just as much today as it was in the days when they enjoyed good health.

Just because their health has diminished, it does not mean that God has diminished or lost His ability to heal, save, restore and deliver them from the illness and into the power of His presence. Faith agrees with God. What He wills is best after all; death is swallowed up in the victory of life.

Death is only a
transition chamber;
it is a common denominator
among all mankind.

Chapter 13

THE CHALLENGE TO LIVE FOREVER

*P*roviding effective presence to the terminally ill assures them of eternal life. They can have hope and remain positive even in this terminal condition. Death has no dominion over their life. Death is not the end of the issue, but a stepping stone from one galley of glory to the next. The life of the believer is graded as an incline, moving from one level of life intensity to the next. Death does not rule, it doesn't govern the life of the believer; but is governed by the giver of all life. The believer lives to live again, the power of death has been destroyed and intentional support assists the patient in keeping a living view of eternal life during the terminal illness and even facing death. The appointment we all have with death is not our last appointment of the day, but rather it is simply an appointment carried over to a better day. We are assured of life and death, and although not desired, it is not feared or final.

Growing up in West Baltimore in a family of seven children, we were challenged. There wasn't always enough of everything to go around. As children, we learned early to be grateful, for such as we had and whatever was lacking didn't prevent us from being happy children. My brothers and I had wonderful adventures, as boys often do. We were *king of the mountain* on one day and *dragon slayers* on the next. When one day ended we knew the next day would be another great adventure. As children we did not fear that tomorrow would not come. God often refers to us as little children to remind us we are relational with Him as our Father. As little children we are encouraged to come to Him and to be dependent upon Him, believing He will and does all that He promises. We may have had natural fathers who didn't keep their word sometimes because situations came up that were outside their control, but we continued to love and trust them. How much more should it be with our heavenly Father who controls all things? The power of death is destroyed by life eternal.

The resurrection of the Body is a truth of doctrine explained in detail by the teachings of the Apostle Paul. The initial principle is to understand what the apostle meant when he used the Greek word for body [SOMA]. It is one of the key words often used by the apostle. In the original Bible language, [SOMA] is a body, an organized whole made up of parts and members that are connected and interdependent. The concept is depicted in plants, celestial and terrestrial bodies, such as the sun, moon and stars. The whole is the body which is comprised of units, members that coexist to provide functionality. Many of Paul's writings and much of his theology include this body imagery. According to Paul it is from the body of sin and death that we are redeemed. It is through the body of Christ on the Cross that we are saved. It is into His body, the Church, that we are incorporated. It is by His body, in the Eucharist, that this fellowship is built and fortified. It is a transforming of our body to the likeness of His glorious body that we are destined for in our eternal existence.

Simplistically we are a part of a greater whole; we are incorporated into the Body of Christ through the life and life giving of Christ. Just as our bodies have within the cell structure the ability to regenerate and replenish over specified periods of time, so in the [SOMA] of Christ is the ability to renew when death comes. The psalmist compares us to the sheep of His pasture and from our beginning in faith we believe we have come from God and so in eventuality we will return to Him. As sons we are being drawn back to the housing of our Father. In John 17:4-5 Jesus says He has finished the work He was assigned and is on His way home. Jesus rightly says "all power is given unto me in heaven and in earth." He further explains His crucifixion as no man having the power to take His life. He announces He has by choice and freedom of will, laid down His life to redeem ours.

Being an older brother myself, I understand the concept of forfeiting what is yours for younger children. I understand the concept of overseeing and being sure the younger children's needs are met. At some time or another we all have put aside our own desires for the needs of our parents, spouse, children and siblings. Jesus' choice to lay down His life for us gave us the gift of life eternal. Now, because of His willful and specific giving, demonstrating God's love, we don't have to fear what any power has over us. We have become in Him a part of the whole of His [SOMA] body. We are connected to one another by our God connection in Christ and because He lives we live. Since death was defeated by Him we have inherited His victory. Death has no power over our living.

The doctrine of the resurrection of the Body is the doctrine of the redemption and replacement of one life by another. The body of our old mortality is replaced by our newness as the body of Christ. The body of death is replaced by the body of life. It is a truth no individual can be saved apart from the whole and the whole doesn't exist outside of Christ. Through His body we are connected and linked with life eternal, where the power of death is destroyed, being made ineffective and void of power. Death cannot extinguish the light of Christ in us. There is no redemption or power available outside of being plugged into the source of life. The darkness of death cannot put out the life or light of Christ in us. The Christian gospel is not the rescuing of individuals out of nature and history; neither does it afford us to escape every trail that humanity endures. Afflictions, trials, temptations and even terminal illness try our humanity; however we are redeemed into a new heaven and new earth, the city of our God, the Body of Christ.

The language of the Apostle Paul is strong concerning the transformation of one's body at death and our receipt of another body. Paul, in his First Corinthian letter, chapter 15, speaks of mortality putting on immortality and corruption putting on incorruption and these bodies of ours shall be transformed in a time frame identified by Paul as a twinkling of an eye. The natural body will return to the earth, because it is natural or of nature. The spiritual body [SOMA] will live on eternally. Flesh and blood, humanity cannot enter that place of eternal peace referred to as Utopia, the *Beulah Land*. These broken down, battered bodies will be exchanged for bodies of great glory and holy magnificence. Paul is fair with us in letting us know that it is all a mystery to Him. He does not know how God is going to do it but he is assured He will do it. Even Moses knew the secret things of God still belong to God, yet what has been revealed belong to us.

It is by and through faith that God starts to reveal Himself to us and we have available to us His revealed will. He begins to etch or write His words and truths in our hearts and in our being. This is the ammunition we have available to us in the times of testing, trials, sickness and even death. We can rest in the promises and power of God who now is working in us through His Holy Spirit. His will for us becomes greater than our will for ourselves. Jesus becomes our example of laying down His will for the will of God. Although in death, what He endured was not tasteful to Him (it was a bitter death), the will of the Father was in Him to join His will [SOMA] to Him. Just as the Roman soldiers did not have power over His life although they had some jurisdiction, His will superseded theirs. No man, no authority could take His life because every authority that exists is instituted by God and there is no authority over God. Every governing authority even death is subject to and limited by the supreme power of God. The eternal power of God is still at work even in the failing body of the terminally ill patient.

When we are walking daily in Christ and in His word, no man nor any power can take our lives, it is simply laid down to be picked back up. When faith and trust in God is with one's whole heart, then even in terminal illness, we lean not unto our own understandings. We seek and receive His help and His direction. As we lay our lives down, the greater love of God in Christ renews and resurrects that life into a newness that never fails. It is this greater love which in Jesus Christ laid down his life for us, that can reassure us in the midst of terminal illness. He lays down His life for the friends of God and even more the sons of God. Paul would have all to know there isn't a legitimate reason for the fear of death. **Death is only a transition chamber; it is a common denominator among all mankind.**

Paul writes, "So when this corruptible shall have put on incorruption and this mortal shall have put on immortality, then, shall be brought to pass the saying that is written, Death is swallowed up in victory. O death, where is thy sting? O grave, where is thy victory? The sting of death is sin; and the strength of sin is the law. But thanks be to God, which gives us the victory through our Lord Jesus Christ."

Mortal man cannot know the mind of God but he follows His divine instructions to live according to His will as outlined in His word, the Bible, basic instructions before leaving earth. It may be that our will or what we want is not God's divine will. In such situations our prayer can be, "Lord give us strength to accept your will and transition our will into your will." Adopting this perspective can inspire one to be open to God's will. Ultimate healing from both physical and spiritual pain and suffering can occur. Our faith in God should enable us to surrender to and be open to God's will for our lives. Is this easy? The answer is "No." It is a life work. That is why the sooner we establish our God relationship, the more experience we have turning our will over to His.

The terminally ill patient who accepts Christ during his illness is just as much privileged to eternal life as the person who has lived their entire life in faith. It is never too late to believe and to be saved.

God is sovereign; He is the supreme authority with no other ruler having dominion or authority over Him. He is the Lord Himself almighty and self existent. He created man in His image with a freedom of will. He has not imposed upon man a robot type nature but has allowed him choice to choose or reject His graces. As a child growing up in a less technical world, a mechanical robot was a gift to be desired. It was very limited in its actions and had a hand held control that allowed us to operate it. By pushing a control you could raise the hands or make the feet move forward; it was a greatly desired toy. We are not toys in the hand of God and we don't automatically default into the will of God; we must make life and death choices. These choices are not available to us if we choose not to submit totally with our heart, soul and mind to God. Our choice of salvation is crucial to our eternal existence. It is important to keep awareness of the firm yet gentle voice of faith calling the patient to the reality of life eternal in Christ.

This voice, His word, breaks down and destroys the power of fear which only comes to torment, discourage and destroy the hope of the patient. The unfailing and eternal love of God restores, revives and resurrects the faith life. The resurrection of Christ from death was His triumphant and victorious march over the power of death. When the false or unreal has been revealed the authentic power and glory of God can be embraced as strength in weakness and transition the patient from life to greater life. It is these truths that must be continually reiterated to not only give hope, but to minister life in the midst of physical dying. The ominous, foreboding presence and pretense of death is destroyed by God's truth and our relationship with Him through Christ Jesus. The knowledge of who we are because of Christ and the victory we walk in gives strength to the terminally ill during this battle. The patient is freed from the tyranny of evil's diabolical scheme to cheat them out of life through fear. They are free to live every moment eternally in the presence of a very present God.

The God life which is now ours in Christ is the real life and not some theater production of an imaginary life; it is the image of God in us. As children we played soldiers fighting one battle after another against imaginary armies and we always won. Every day the terminally ill are in a battle for life naturally and physically and we can assure them they will always win too. We are daily walking in a victory already won. The spoils of war are our eternal life in Christ. We cheer from the finish line reminding the faithful on the other side there is a winner's circle and a crown of life. We are not rushing the patient to the finish line but preparing and reminding them once they cross it, there will be joys unthinkable and eternal. This is fuel for the fight today, to hold on during the battle and keep the faith once delivered to us as war heroes returning home.

No matter how microscopic or myopic our vision and hope is, we may discover that some knowledge is not revealed to us.

Chapter 14

LIFE CHALLENGED BY INDUSTRY AND PROGRESS

*D*id you know that many accidents happen at home, in our safe or familiar environment? Isn't it strange to think that we accidentally fall, slip or injure ourselves in the most familiar and supposedly safe environments? We are getting out of the shower, the mat we usually step on is out of place and we fall. The familiar is out of place. We are going down the stairs as we do every day and suddenly we simply miss the step. We are getting out of the car in our driveway carrying packages and stumble, injuring our knee. We drop a glass in our kitchen and it breaks. After sweeping up all the broken pieces we step barefooted and still cut our foot. Are these accidents simply accidents or were they preventable? Can we safe proof our homes to make them less accident prone or can we safe proof our lives so accidents never happen? It may well be that no matter how careful we are we still have the occasional accidents.

History evidences that most of us will endure some type of sickness preceding death. It is the addition and subtraction clause of life. Although we may have a longer life expectancy today than in the generations preceding us, it is subject to the mathematics of life. We have many life extending medical advancements to help us live longer and healthier. They include supplements, age deterring drugs, cosmetic enhancements and safer house and home building products. The extended days, as stated in Psalms 90:10, may well be full of trouble; however, with modern advancement we have given ease to much of it. Yet with all the advances in technology and product development we still experience many deaths and terminal illnesses at early ages, such as cancer, end-stage renal failure, lupus, Multiple Sclerosis, HIV and AIDS, Parkinson, Hodgkin's disease, Alzheimer's, Menincocco Meningitis and congestive heart failure.

In the same manner we have different reflections or reasons for the causes of terminal illness being present in our lives. We can keep ourselves abreast of all the current medical advantages and preventive care and still see terminal illness in our lifetime. We may question from where does terminal illness come. What is its origin? Can persons avoid it or escape it? Are we destined for an encounter with a terminal illness? Is it possible that even our familiar places, the places where our families reside or frequent, have potentially dangerous influences? If we were to take a poll of randomly selected persons, it is probable that the answers, commentaries and opinions generated by such questioning would cover a wide spectrum of responses. We believe, if we know the cause, we can affect the result, which is often true. Every cause however is not revealed to us and every remedy is not available to us. Each generation has its own enlightenment, its progress and certainly its knowledge, yet all knowledge is not and never will be available to us in our humanity.

No matter how microscopic or myopic our vision and hope is, we may discover that some knowledge is not revealed to us. From a general perspective, medical professionals will agree that the source of terminal illness can have its roots in a lack of proper medical attention, the gross negligence of health maintenance and preventive measures. The excessiveness of our generation is often reflected in alcohol binging, drugs (legal or illegal) and inhalants (whether smoking or pollution). The preoccupation with cosmetics and enhancements that influence and invade our everyday lives can reflect our respectability in propagating terminal illness. Improper eating habits, including fast foods with too many fatty acids, highly seasoned foods, a large intake of cholesterols and sugars can be serious contributors to terminal illness. The lack of a routine exercise program is also a contributor to our receptiveness to terminal illness. Medical professionals further state that stress, domestic, social or job related, can contribute to a terminal illness. Substances that change or interrupt the natural functions of the body can be attributed to terminal illnesses.

Terminal illness for some is thought to be the natural order of things that cannot be avoided or escaped. It is after all in our DNA, in our family history. The 21st century man is completely dependent upon industry and bureaucracy to feed him. The food we eat is processed with chemicals, fertilizers and many types of drugs producing a quick growth. Vegetables and animals no longer go through the natural growing process, which would entail time and care. Greed and lower costs of development or care cause the industry to claim that without the use of these unnatural elements, the natural process would not allow them to produce the volume demanded by the public. Often the industry claims that without the chemicals and drugs the world would starve due to overpopulation and lack of farmland. Again, industry has taken much of the open land developing it for housing and amusement. It takes three to four weeks for a chick to develop into an adult chicken, but with additives included in the feed of the chick it can develop in five to seven days. With the use of chemicals the growth processing has been increased many times over. This small elementary example is representative of most of the foods we eat, be it meat or vegetable.

I have taken the time to become more familiar with food processing, engaging in dialogue with persons who have exposed me to studies of the chemicals used to process food for human consumption. Processes such as fertilizing the ground, spraying vegetation with chemicals to control pestilent insects and rodents and also soil enhancements affect our consumption of unhealthy products. Preservatives are commonly used to sustain the harvest. They allow fresh food to be eaten long after it is picked or prepared and frozen food to be consumed many months after processing. Preservatives make food appear healthy and enticing because they cause food to last longer. We are eating foods that have been injected with dyes and chemicals. This knowledge should alarm us, making us aware that the price paid by humanity is far greater than the benefits. In some cases, we have saved a few minutes of cooking time and shortened our life expectancy.

The levels of chemicals in our foods are so high that the food itself has been robbed of its natural nutrients. One does not have to be a genius to identify the profit making element present in the food industry. The faster you can produce, the longer the shelf life of the product, the more profit the industry can gain. It may be that the giants in the food industry have pledged a secret alliance to make certain that nothing changes even if it means that persons consuming unhealthy foods are experiencing terminal illnesses in greater numbers. Although the average life span is increasing, there is also an increase in the number of cancer victims. It is like the patch theory; we patch one whole to discover another. If we want healthy lengthy lives we may have to forego quick producing and fast marketing schemes to achieve it.

Research done by health specialists and nutritionists Dick Gregory and Ralph Nader and others report that the foods we eat are killing us because of the high levels or the presence of chemicals. One of the causes of cancer, a leading disease classified as terminal illness, is believed to be the many deposits of chemicals in our bodies. Over the years, the chemicals collected in our bodies from the foods eaten will begin to have a negative effect. Cancer is terminal because there isn't a consistent or confirmed cure. There is treatment; however the treatment requires consistent monitoring and retreatment. Years ago when life was simple, even though it was time consuming, our food was healthier. We grew our vegetables and fed our animals the best grain and feed available. There were no chemical fertilizers and chemical pesticides. We were secure in the natural order of things. We waited for the chicken to develop and lay eggs. Our food was not filled with chemical additives. Our food was prepared naturally and prepared foods were not as easily accessible. Yesterday's generations did not face the kind of sicknesses and illnesses we are faced with today in such large numbers. Certainly terminal illness always existed but not as readily as we see today. America today is dependent upon an industry and bureaucracy to keep food on the table. America is not necessarily as health conscious as it was in yesteryear.

Excessive use of over the counter medicines for the alleviation of symptoms keeps many self medicating and disregarding the warning labels. This is also seen as cost effective to avoid costly physician's visits and prescription drugs. When reading the labels of drugs and the PDR [Physician's Desk Reference] for medications, you will notice the adverse reactions to the pharmaceutical drugs. Because of the nutrients missing in our diet, the use and abuse of vitamins and dietary supplements together have generated a decrease in our immune system. The rising cost of produce makes it more cost effective to dine on burgers from the value menu. Our jobs and family schedules make it also more convenient to grab a quick fast food burger. We are accustomed to getting something on the go and eating fast food. In a computer generated society with all information just a mouse click away, we have to make an effort to exercise. One can work an entire day without moving from the desk, promoting many forms of arthritis and muscular and nerve disorders. With a concentration on the cosmetics of life, we consume more protein energy bars and caffeine drinks to give us energy and control our hunger. Fashion will also promote a less than healthy weight and encourages weight gain surgeries to make the change needed to fit in or enhance or quickly remove the excess or unwanted areas. We can plump our lips and shrink our hips in one visit.

Because of the population explosion and the challenges of living in a global society, man has found that his technological advances in the food processing cycle have not always benefitted humanity. Man has become his own worst enemy. The water we drink, the water used for cooking and bathing is believed to be contaminated causing or giving rise to certain terminal illness. The water we drink contains chemicals thought to be purifiers. But once again our bodies, through the consumption of water, are used as depositories for water soluble chemicals. Scientific research will show a relationship between food and water contaminated with chemicals being one of the sources of some terminal illnesses. Officials will be quick to state that all the drugs or chemicals used in food and water are harmless. Many autopsies show that over the years, the deposits built up within the cell walls and cell tissues of the human body are the real causes of some terminal illnesses. Thus, it strongly suggests that these chemicals and drugs used in our food and water are anything but harmless. In fact, the real truth is that they may be more harmful than we realize.

Even medical treatment in the form of excessive radiology screening is now being investigated as creating an overexposure of the body to harmful radiation; thus adding to the causes of terminal illnesses. Medical professionals, having realized the advanced technology in the food processing industry and its profit making motives foster little or no real effort or desire to return to simple agricultural practices of the food processing of yesterday. Medical professionals also realize that the demand for food is of such a great magnitude that it is probably impossible to talk about a return to normal growth times. Farming is no longer a lucrative vocation and land is at a premium as real estate. Most of the foods that we eat are warehoused or green housed. Our oceans, rivers and streams are polluted and contaminated with chemical waste, oil spills and drugs that are contributing to the rise of terminal illnesses. Even the air we breathe is full of pollution and toxic poisoning which directly contributes to terminal illness. The search for alternative sources for fuel may help the over pollution of the air we breathe.

As detailed here there are many contributors to terminal illness. As we understand some of the many contributors to becoming terminally ill, we also better understand some of the cause agents. We can view our ability to escape terminal illness or its influences as impossible. However no matter how good or how bad the effects of agricultural, chemical and medical advances are, we must not walk in fear and pessimism. In the sorting of details, behavior patterns and mistakes of yesterday, one should never forget the presence of God nor discount the power of God. The person who is struggling in sickness, suffering and whose body is stripped of ease will need to pull on the knowledge of God and His workings to deal with their pain. Life appears to be leaving minute by minute and yet it is also being renewed day by day. Again, do not leave God out of the equation, out of the healing process even when the diagnosis is terminal. Faith is a key component in the treatment of the terminally ill.

Many view a terminal illness as the natural order of things. Sickness and terminal illness is a part of man's imperfection and greed. Because of man's disobedience to God's will, he was evicted from paradise. Disobedience and sinfulness in man didn't allow him to live any longer under the blanket coverage and perfection he once knew in paradise. Many may view terminal illness as a purifying of the soul through suffering to release it from an eternal punishment. We often, like the friends of Job, are limited in our understanding of the nature of God and we talk eternal matters from a limited perspective and understanding. The wisdom of man is foolishness with God, but it can be hurtful to the terminally ill. Whatever the cause, the terminally ill live with the result of the illness daily. The ministry of "PRESENCE" is a ministry to the present situation of the terminally ill to give hope and assistance to the patients and their families.

Man's confirmed appointment with death and his confirmed appointment with sickness (which many times lead to death) is seen throughout the Bible. Job reminds us in the fourteenth chapter that, "that born of woman is full of trouble and of few days. Naked we came into this world and naked we shall return." The Word of God provides a continual reminder that the Christian has a return ticket, validated by the Lord. The ticket grants entry into the holiness and wholeness of God. There is a prepared place for prepared people and the welcome mat is always laid out for those who have given their life and hope to God. Even in the pain and distress of terminal illness the patient is not alone when in faith. God is a responder to the earnest cry of the believer and His ever present bedside gives hope and life today and forever.

Sickness maybe inevitable; as we live, we are propelled closer to the clutches of death. Terminal illness maybe a natural process; it may move us closer to this concept of our returning to dust. It can be understood as moving us closer to the awareness that we no longer exist in a perfect paradise of life and life more abundantly in a physical sense.

Some terminal illnesses occur as a result of the over exertion of the human body. The body becomes worn and torn down. The heart is overworked; veins and arteries become restricted and proper blood flow to provide nutrients for cells is impaired. The colon, toxic with waste material over the years, can become cancerous. Terminal illnesses can come from a variety of events, circumstances and unique situations. A grandmother and a grandfather announcing a diagnosis of inoperable cancer after 75 years of life isn't as shocking as a young person, not yet 10 years old, having the same diagnosis. Senior citizens suffering from Alzheimer's disease, forgetting how to do things they have been doing all their lives and forgetting the names of loved ones is seen as simply growing old. But when it happens at 20 or 30 years old, is it viewed as part of the natural order? Today if one lives long enough, one will experience sickness. A terminal illness may become a reality.

The 90th Psalm further declares that death is so certain that our lives have already been forecasted for confrontation with death. *"We live our lives as a tale that is already told. The days of our years are three score years and ten and if by reason of strength they be four score years, yet it is with labor and sorrow, for it is soon cut off and we fly away. So teach us to number our days that we may apply our hearts unto wisdom."* The psalmist recognizes the heart will one day cease its activities and the lungs will take a final rest. Blood will not travel through the veins and arteries and when that time comes, death will be at hand. Regardless of the years spent on the earth, the accomplishments and the pleasures experienced, this life will come to an end. The appointment with death is inevitable if the Lord does not come in our lifetime.

Yet the promise of eternal life is the champion that meets the challenge. Life is just as sure if not more certain than death. Those who have put their trust in God can be assured that no matter what life brings in its final stages, there is an abundance of life; diseases are rendered powerless and are defeated.

Terminal illness is not always
based upon or the result of
the lifestyle of the patient.

Chapter 15

THE CHALLENGE
OF MISCONCEPTIONS

My choice of vocation before being called into ministry was to be a physician. I began preparing myself early by looking into the causes of the matter of illness and having compassion for the sick. In the study of biology and chemistry you are required to take a close, microscopic view of things that would go unseen by the naked eye. You have to search for the cause underneath the symptoms and commonality of a disease. Although multiple symptoms may appear, often the central cause is usually one specific illness. The hard job is trying to differentiate or separate the symptoms from the illness. The same holds true when we take a close look at what the Bible has to say about terminal illness. We will discover a variety of instances of terminal illness and many causes. All of them may not fit into our understanding of the Christian life. The Bible describes the history of God reaching out to humanity. The etymology of that history discloses a progressive development, with respect to man's understanding, of what it means to be God's people.

To prepare to become a physician it requires commitment to years of study and exposure to the frailties and possibilities of death, regardless of medical intervention. All illness cannot be attributed to a life pattern or a family history. Certainly these can be contributing factors to the illness but is not always considered the primary cause. Everyone diagnosed with a specific illness will not have the same response to treatment. Some diseases have a greater mortality rate than others. There are certain behaviors that will put a person at medical risk for specific diseases; however they are not always the cause of the disease itself. There will be people who do not exhibit a negative behavior pattern and still become terminally ill. There will be those whose negative behavior pattern can be attributed to the cause of their terminal illness. **Terminal illness is not always based upon or the results of the lifestyle of the patient.**

People do not always view terminal illness as the natural order of life but have identified terminal illness as being punishment for one's sin or disobedience to God's will. Some believe that the person who suffers with Alzheimer's suffers because they had a misspent youth or lived a mean, rotten, sinful life. They believe that God's punishment for them as a senior citizen is suffering without reasoning. This same person who believes a terminal illness is the punishment of one's sins, either public or private, may also say that the homosexual or the drug addict who is an intravenous user and who has contracted AIDS or who is HIV positive, is sick because it is God's punishment. They believe that people who have defiled their bodies and not presented them holy and acceptable to God are now stricken by God. How easily we attribute humanistic reasoning to the workings of God who is infinitely wise and whose ways are above our ability to reason. Why some and not all sinners would be punished in this manner is never made clear.

The Bible provides insights and considerations for this very narrow view. Historically in the earliest stages of the development, we can see a cause and effect disclosure of sin and God's vengeance upon evil doers. God's relationship with His people was expressed in the law of the Old Testament. If a man were faithful to that law, he could expect health and prosperity as a reward. If he was unfaithful, then God would punish him with sickness and misfortune. This action and reaction was a principle demonstration and teaching of man's accountability to God. The teaching included the all powerfulness of God and man's need to fear or reverence Him as the all powerful or almighty God. It was quite simplistic. If you do well, then you can expect good. If you do evil, expect the same. It is a basic, even simple "cause and effect" teaching, which is similar to how we teach our children, the reward or punish method. The same is often true in medical treatment. We isolate the bacteria, virus or malignancy and attempt to kill it without destroying the patient.

The first Psalm expresses how a faithful Israelite expected to be treated by God:

Happy is the Man

Who never follows the advice of the wicked

Or loiters on the way that sinners take

Or sits about with scoffers

But finds his pleasure in the law of the Lord

And meditate on his law day and night

He is like a tree that is planted

By the waters streams

Yielding fruit in due season

Its leaves never fading.

Success attends all he does.

It is nothing like the wicked,

No, these are like chaff blown away by the wind.

The wicked will not stand, when judgment comes.

Nor sinners, when the virtuous assemble.

For the Lord takes care of the virtuous, but the way of

the wicked is doomed.

It was simply an expectation of earthly reward and punishment. The idea of a life after death or a heaven for reward and a hell for punishment, would not develop for a long time. Because of this expectation, the Israelites often figured that sickness and pain were the just deserts of the sinner, especially people who caused trouble for the faithful. For that reason they would sometimes pray quite sincerely for disaster to befall their enemies:

> *May their own table prove a trap for them,*
> *And their plentiful suppliers a snare.*
> *May their eyes grow dim, go blind*
> *Strike their loins with chronic palsy.*
> *(Psalm 69:22-23)*

On the other hand, it was not a surprise for the person who knew he had sinned against the law to find himself sick. A Psalm describes the plight of such a sinner as be begs forgiveness:

> *No soundness in my flesh now you are angry*
> *No health in my bones, because of my sin.*
> *My guilt is overwhelming me,*
> *It is too heavy a burden.*
> *My wounds stick and are festering*
> *The result of my folly*
> *Bowed down, bent double, overcome*
> *I go mourning all the day*
> *(Psalm 38:3-6)*

This is a lament, but not a complaint. The sinner recognized his guilt and accepted the consequences. He only hoped to be restored and to prove anew his fidelity to the law. The different ideas about sickness and its underlying causes revealed a deepening of one's understanding of their own suffering and a gradual awakening to the meaning of that suffering in their relationship with God.

It might appear that this view of sickness is an arbitrary punishment imposed on man by a vengeful God. Indeed some people view sickness that way even today. However, there was a deeper insight here, the recognition that sickness and sin are somehow closely related and that sickness is a particularly appropriate result of sin. Sickness, as articulated in the early Bible, accounts as a collision with human limitations. Sickness is a harsh reminder of the reality of man's finiteness, his liability to death. Sickness pricks the balloon of human pride and evaporates the illusion that man can get along fine if left to his own devices. The wise Israelite recognized that the wicked man, the proud man, got just the medicine he earned when sickness struck and forced him to his human limits. Therefore, sickness was the sign or evidence of sin or a life lived in trespass. Sickness was the symbol of the true condition of a man left to his own resources, apart from God. On the other hand, the faithful acknowledged they owed their prosperity, their meaning and wholeness to God. The prayer, sacrifice and careful observance of the law expressed that attitude. This provided a kind of insurance against needing the lesson taught by sickness.

From this Bible history we can see how terminal ill-nesses was and is still considered by many to be God's punishment for persons who have sinned against His will. Good health, perfect health and old age were signs of one who is faithful and obedient to God. The persons enjoying "the good life" are persons who are considered holy and righteous in God's sight. The person whose health was less than perfect was thought to be a sinful person, a person working against the will of God. The penalty for working against God was once viewed by some Bible readers as the cause of sickness. This inter-pretation of sin in relationship to sickness is most in-teresting and has continued for some even to this day.

This concept of earned benefits makes the grace of God of no effect. We would still be under the dictates of living according to the law, but the law could not and did not redeem mankind. Our relationship with God would be based upon self-righteousness and being human. We would become prideful that it is our good works, our own perfectness that keeps us in good health. Any illness or sickness would be evidence to the world that there was a sin factor in our lives. If that sick-ness ended in death that was even more evidence of a life lived in sin.

The Bible again sheds some light on this concern, a light that empowers readers of the word to find handles of clarification. The people of God attempted to live according to this view of sickness, with its simple expectation of earthly reward and punishment. However, they noticed some disturbing inconsistencies. For example, a number of flagrantly wicked people were ignoring God's law and doing quite well for themselves in the process. They lived successful and prosperous lives, enjoying good health. They lived to a good age without any noticeable consequence of their apparent wickedness. There appeared to be an inequity in the response of God to wickedness. The prophet Jeremiah respectfully questioned God about that:

"You have right on your side, Lord; when I complained about you. But I would like to debate a point of justice with you. Why is it that the wicked live so prosperously? Why do scoundrels enjoy peace? You plant them, they take root and flourish and even bear fruit." (Jeremiah 12:1-4)

The questions were even more disturbing when the faithful asked, *"Why do the wicked prosper, while the righteous suffer?"* The question arises as a crisis of faith and every crisis of faith must be dealt with immediately lest the faithful fall into faithlessness. The words of inquiry will soon turn to accusations of injustice and unreliability in God's actions and reactions to sin. This questioning goes to the root of the concept of good to those doing good and sickness and destruction to those who live wickedly. The integrity of God is questionable when the hypostasis of only good coming to those doing well is challenged when the wicked enjoy good. It confounds the understanding of the righteous good and the sovereignty of God becomes questionable. After all, look at them; these are the wicked, well off and still getting richer! *After all, why should I keep my own heart pure and wash my hands in innocence, if you plague me all day long and discipline me every morning?*

Another disturbing inconsistency was the shadow of guilt that sickness cast on a faithful man. If God rewards the faithful and punishes the unfaithful with sickness and you happen to be sick, there is one clear conclusion that people could draw. You have been secretly unfaithful to God and have participated in sin behind closed doors or in discreet places. You have committed some hidden sin, but now it is revealed for all, by your illness. The gossip at this point runs wild with speculation, wanting to narrow down the actual sin cause. Now added to the terminal illness is the concept that you have hidden some insidious sin that is the cause of the illness plaguing you. The simple comforts and concerns of those around you are not available to you because they view your illness as the action of God's judgment in the affairs of man. Simply stated the terminally ill may be getting what secret sin has warranted them. If they can locate the sin virus and turn from it, their health will be restored.

This way of thinking was prevalent, even in the New Testament times. It surfaced in Christ's followers as they confronted a blind man. They asked, *"Rabbi, who sinned, this man or his parents for him to have been born blind?"* The Master responded, *"Neither has sinned, but that my father in heaven might be glorified." (John 9:1-12)* This response was quite confusing to the disciples. They were steeped in Jewish tradition. They were familiar with the laws as they related to sickness. The prophecies of yesterday declared that, *"because of the sour grapes eaten by generations before, generations unborn would experience suffering for previous sins" (Ezekiel 18:2).* The Master knew He was being challenged historically and traditionally in that He was being asked by His disciples about sin and the persons who would pay the penalty for sin. He responded masterfully and in a manner that refuted Jewish tradition and history. Here we find sickness portrayed as an opportunity for man to experience the glory and greatness of God as opposed to being the result of sin. The response evidenced neither, but for the manifestation of God's glory; he was blind.

The book of Job is almost exclusively concerned with this disturbing inconsistency. Job, an unquestionably just man, is terribly sick. He asks himself, his friends and his God, *"Why must a just man suffer illness?"* His friends concluded that whether he realized it or not, he must have sinned. This was a logical concept as it relates to the understanding of that time. Job had three friends who were convinced that he was sick because he had sinned against God. Eliphas, remarked, *"A guilty conscience prompts your words."* Elihu remarked, *"Do you presume to maintain that you are in the right, to insist on your innocence before God?"* In spite of their remarks, Job persisted to raise disturbing questions until finally he realized that the simple expectation of earthly rewards and punishments, dependent upon man's righteous or unrighteousness, completely undermined the old view of sickness as a punishment from God.

Man could simply be a law abiding citizen and be rewarded and this expectation made the relationship between God and man too simple. All a person had to do was to observe the law and God would be almost bound to make life pleasant for him. Man would have a sense of rightness in himself and no real relationship to God. This expectation forgot that God is transcendent, completely beyond the limits of human understanding and the reach of human powers. It assumed that men should make a legal claim against God and haul God into court in a sort of civil suit. They could present their cause to God and make Him accountable to be just and equitable based upon their record of legal compliance.

Job could not understand why God would cause him to experience unthinkable suffering. Job complained to God. In fact, he asked for a court hearing, with God as the defendant. In the majestic violence of a storm God showed Job his mistake and confronted him with the truth about his human condition. God said, "Who is this obscuring my design, with his empty words: Let me ask you questions and it is your answer to me! Tell me, since you are so wise! Have you ever in your life given orders to the morning? Or sent the dawn to melt the darkness? Whose command set down the laws of the heavens and plotted the course of the stars? Can your voice carry as far as the clouds and make the thunder and rain do your bidding? Who stretches his hand over the cold earth to bring forth the buds and blossoms of spring? Or do you really want to accuse me and put me in the wrong to put yourself in the right?" (*Job 38:1-7*)

As God spoke and challenged Job's intelligence, in his logical thinking Job soon realized that he was no earthly opponent for God. Job clearly understood, while in the midst of his personal suffering and tribulation, with his body crying out for immediate relief, that he had no legitimate right to question or to challenge the will of God. He specifically realized that his intelligence was infinitely inferior to God's. Job realized how absurd it was for man to dream he should make demands and accusations against God. It was equally absurd for man to think he could bargain with or try to manipulate God to feel obligated to man. Job now speaks in the context of humility in the revelation of truth:

"I know that you are all-powerful, what you conceive, you can perform. I am the man who obscured your designs with my empty words. I have been holding forth on matters I cannot understand or marvels beyond me and my knowledge. I knew you then, only by hear-say, but now, having seen you with my own eyes, I retract all I have said and in dust and ashes I repent."

Viewing Job through the window of sin and sickness does not explain the Job experience. His whole view of sickness as a punishment for sin, evaporated like a fog before the warm and brilliant majesty of God. Job learned God's designs are sometimes inscrutable; but since God is faithful, he faithfully can trust in God's love and accept whatever befalls them.

The ministry of 'Presence" brings the comfort of a loving God and not an angry judgmental God who is punishing the terminally ill for pass sins. The immutability and integrity of God cannot be challenged by the understanding or misconceptions of man. The terminal illness is not God's judgment and does not indicate His punishment. As we have previously discussed there are many reasons why illness comes. Some positive actions on our part can help us resist them but it doesn't guarantee illnesses will not affect us. Terminal illness is not evidence of sin or God's displeasure. We can better minister to the needs of the terminally ill when we better understand the nature and character of God.

Faith is a confidence
beyond a simple belief;
it is trusting in God's integrity.

SECTION IV: THE TRUTH SHALL MAKE YOU FREE

Chapter 16

THE TRUTH WE LIVE TO HEAR

As I go through my exercise regiment daily whether on the treadmill or pressing weights to maintain good physical condition, I am confident that while my physical body is increasing in its overall effectiveness, my brain is producing and releasing endorphins. Those endorphins are natural pain relievers helping my body absorb the stress and discomfort of the exercise. Busy people often forget the necessity of exercise in their daily schedule. Regular exercise has been shown to improve the brain functions, relieve stress and may even guard against dementia. Consistent exercise may also increase levels of "brain-derived neurotrophic factor" (BDNF) which can improve your mood. This is apparent to me because, after a good exercise I feel better. Although tired, I am invigorated. The whole time I am putting my body through my daily exercise course of pulling, straining and lifting, my mind is eliminating stresses and my body pain is eased. There are days when I simply don't feel like exercising; but because I know the benefits of it, I push myself past my feelings to condition my body and release my mind to its benefit. I know the stresses of the day are better endured, my energy level heightened and my attitude calm when I take the time to exercise. I become healthier in mind and spirit. I am encouraged and many negative responses are avoided when I take the time to maintain a regular exercise schedule. Therefore, I have concluded, regardless of the immediate discomfort of bodily exercise, it increases my effectiveness physically, mentally and emotionally.

It is when we become more knowledgeable of the Bible (as a whole and not in parts and pieces) that our view of sickness and terminal illness changes. No longer is a historical view or even a limited present day view of terminal illness as punishment acceptable. Rather, we know terminal illness is a part of the living experience of man. We are not always given all the answers to the dilemmas of humankind or the conditions that are a part of the dealings of God with and in His people. Every activity and action is not revealed or understood by us as there are still the secret things of God. We have, however, been promised His presence. It is with us in every situation of life and we will never be abandoned. As the historical biblical views change and as knowledge increases, man's relational awareness and confidence of God's presence has also increased.

Just as my morning exercise increases, so does my endurance level. I endure, keeping my goal in sight. Growing in the knowledge of God helps us endure, accept and have confidence in what once seemed in our limited view, a punishment. We begin to see beyond our prior shortsightedness, which limited God to only being the guarantor of earthly happiness and one who insures and supports our dreams. God's purpose for humanity is beyond the understanding of man's preconceived notions and perceptions. God's ways, methods and purposes are not all revealed today. Some are concealed to be known at a later date. Yet, we can be confident that He is at work within the lives of humans for the purpose of drawing people to a deeper and purer awareness of Him. This drawing into a deeper awareness will bring us to a satisfaction beyond our earlier expectations and concepts.

God has retained undisclosed information not yet revealed, that has not been shared and belongs to Him alone, as indicated in Deuteronomy 29:29. Everything about God or His plan for us is not always explained. During times when we don't understand, faith is essential. **Faith is a confidence beyond a simple belief; it is trusting in God's integrity.** He will always do what is beneficial to man even when we don't understand the route He takes or the purpose of our journey. Every day we are in the keeping power and authority of God. We realize that sickness is not a measuring rod for one's sinfulness. Some people even view sickness as an opportunity to exercise their faith. It is in the moments of the deepest tragedies, as in the 9/11 terrorist attacks, that men drew aside and pulled closer to God, even those who had resisted Him the most. Remember the scenes of government officials standing in prayer during the 9/11 terrorist crises?

Many persons have discovered a genuine personal faith encounter and a lasting relationship with God through the experience of terminal illness. Suffering and sickness by some was viewed as an initiation into a special faith relationship in order to reach the profound insight into the overall life design called wisdom. This is a type of penitence or religious rigor that would bring about divine revelation. In this broader interpretation of sickness, it was no longer laced with fear and guilt, but colored with loving patience and a new kind of expectation. Sickness was viewed as the mark of a faith relationship and it bore the promise of being called into a deeper and more pure realization of that relationship. The rewards expected were no longer easily identifiable resources of the earth. They were the gifts of God that were to come with spiritual fullness and also through suffering.

It is very important that the patient who is enduring terminal illness is able to interpret their situation in a positive and not punishing light. It is necessary for those in constant contact with the patient to develop a positive approach and interpretation of their health situation.

The Bible instructs us not to sit in unnecessary judgment of one another but to encourage one another. We can argue theoretically about the origin of illness and the fall of man, however none of us is exempt from illness. We can disagree regarding the cause of terminal illness, however just as the discomfort of the daily routine has a positive result, we must also communicate that regardless of the toll and severity of the terminal illness, *all things still work together for good for those who love the Lord and are the called according to His purpose.*

"Presence" comes as a stabilizing agent to reassure the patient of God's continual care and strength being active and available during the illness. Such assistance and companionship encourages the patient to receive God by faith and allow God to participate in their recovery process. Active faith will help guide the patient. They are not alone; God is with them in their daily struggle for life. God's presence can become visible in the demonstration of kindness, consistency, care and the presence of helpers and companions during this important time in the life of the patient. God will be present through His effectual working, patience and preparation of a prepared ministry to the terminally ill.

Today we live in a highly technological society; there are laptops, notebooks, camcorders fitting in our palms, fax machines, high definition TV, iPads, iPhones and many more technical advances. There is an abundance of television preacher personalities that can be viewed on most major television networks. The gospel can ride the winds of the satellite and television, exposing many to the salvation words of God. It helps to turn lives away from destruction to a constructive relationship with God. However some of these personalities using television teaching and preaching are persons very limited in their interpretation of God's word. Many are tunnel minded and can only see one narrow view.

With a one dimensional view, many are not open to other possibilities of God at work. Some may well be simply promoting an image or half truths. That can be deceptive and harmful. Some will say, on television, both national and international, "If one is sick it is because one is a sinner. Accept Jesus. Ask Him into your life and be saved and healed." Some will even say, "One is sick because one's faith is weak. Strengthen your faith and your body will be healed." These persons often make statements declaring, a true believer of God's word will never get sick, will never contract cancer, Alzheimer's, AIDS and other terminal disorders." As positive as they may appear, I dare to tell you they are positively misleading and incorrectly representing the Word of God and how He interacts with mankind.

Such rhetoric is dangerous and does not have a sound theological foundation. In the 80's there were strong attitudes and judgments concerning AIDS. Many leaders of large fundamentalist churches, who were also involved in a daily or weekly national broadcast, were asked to give their understanding or interpretation of AIDS as it related to biblical teachings. These fundamentalists television preachers were apologetic with rage. They spoke of AIDS as the gay plague brought down by God to punish homosexuals for their sins. My immediate reaction to watching preachers franticly respond to what they could not understand while attempting to defend God was futile. The question became, "Would Jesus have said these things?" In their vision some sins were by definition, beyond the boundary of the church and are justly deserving of severe retribution. How do we justify such a narrow perspective when Jesus says He came to seek and save the lost? These who were whole did not require a physician but He came for those who were sick. He didn't qualify the level of sickness by disqualifying any one illness as being beyond His scope of relational healing.

This visual spectacle of religious judgment in ministers raving against AIDS was distasteful. Instead of drawing men to faith, it set up road blocks or barriers for many. These faith obstacles prevented many terminally ill patients' access and comfort in their time of crisis. This exhibition showcased Christians a long way from the teachings of faith and mercy. Faith and sound teachings are accessible to anyone and are easy to understand. Jesus made a specific point of working among people rejected by the society of His time. He went to the lepers, who were then feared and rejected more than AIDS patients today. They were publicly pronounced unclean, rejected by all who crossed their paths and were expected to live outside society.

He blessed prostitutes and alcoholics who we would call the dregs or misfits of society. He didn't bless the work they did, but he blessed and shared a message of hope, repentance and salvation with them. He protected the human rights of an adulterer and called men into accountability about their own transgression. There was a reminder that all men are equally guilty and in need of forgiveness. He said, "He that is without sin among you, let him cast the first stone." Jesus taught forgiveness, tolerance, inclusion and above all, love. The only people with whom He became angry were the money lenders in the temple and the Pharisees who were judgmental in their spiritual hearses. His anger was with those who spoke words of condemnation and had no pity or love for the suffering of others, as condemnation was not a part of His doctrine.

In order to effectively develop assistance for the terminally ill, we will need to develop a Christ centric approach in interpretation of terminal illness. Both the historical and traditional view of sickness in the Old

Testament will be insufficient, unproductive for this present age. The marriage between the Old Testament and the New Testament, laced in the understanding of Jesus, can provide us with the tools needed to effectively help those who are terminally ill. We must be willing to serve the lost, sick and destitute with patience and with knowledge. The sensitivity of our faith and kindness is the earmark of those who bring hope and comfort to the terminally ill and their families.

Preaching can be comforting and compassionate to persons who are suffering physically, feeling all alone and forsaken. It can also be comforting for those and who are suffering spiritually, perhaps from unintentional incorrect application of Bible truths. When the future is bleak, hope can be found through the preached word. A source of genuine truth and comfort can make a world of difference to the patient. Preaching is comforting in that it creates an atmosphere of confident assurance. The assurance is in knowing the terminally ill patient is never alone even when the burden of sickness is heavy and aggressive. It is also in the comforting and assurance of the peace and power of God that is ever present. Preaching enforces and makes the statement and promises given thousands of years ago clear concerning an ever present *Comforter*. Preaching cements in the mind of the terminally ill the sincerity of the words "I will not leave you comfortless." Preaching highlights and articulates the open arms of God to receive and forgive.

The apostle Paul aptly said, "I think myself happy." This type of control allows the patient to live on their terms with the terminal illness and opens the door for the healing of God. One can be assured of the risen Christ who has demonstrated authority over death having defeated it. The terminally ill can participate in His victory. A good percentage of the terminally ill is not able to attend church to hear the messages. We are recorders and broadcasters of the hope available right there in the room of the patient. Today we live in a technological age and we can bring faithful and reassuring messages of hope and love to the patient.

While making hospital visits, I met a lady who had been diagnosed with cancer. She was a 53 year old woman, married 23 years to the same man, the mother of four, and one who believed in God but was now confronted with an extreme situation. Her initial reason for being in the hospital was to have her tonsils removed. She had developed a bad case of tonsillitis. Much swelling and irritation had developed to the point that her tonsils were inflamed and needed to be removed. During her stay at the hospital, she was routinely examined for cancer. The test yielded a positive result showing cancerous lumps in both the right and left breast. This finding led to a thorough physical and more extensive testing for the presence of cancer. The results were overwhelming as it proved to be more severe than she imagined. The cancer cells were not only in her breasts, but were actively spreading throughout her body.

She had entered the hospital to have a simple tonsillectomy, which should have been a routine surgical procedure at low risk. Now she has discovered she has cancer that is in the terminal stages. I happened to meet her by just being at the hospital (or was I introduced to her for His purpose). God was at work causing my will to yield to His will because His concern for her was not her illness, but her faith and hope. He will put us on a collision course and in the right place for one another. Her family members, who were visiting the patient, left the patient's room to go to the cafeteria. On the way, one of them recognized me going in the opposite direction. She earnestly asked if I would have prayer and visit her mother (who was the cancer patient). As she briefly explained her mother's condition, I sensed she wanted more than just a simple visit. I was uncertain if the patient had accepted the diagnosis or if she was in denial or a stage of rage. I wasn't even sure if the patient herself wanted prayer. I only knew for sure she was terminally ill and whatever comfort and assurance I could give I was committed and prepared to give.

I prayerfully braced myself and yielded to the request

of the daughter. I soon found myself in the hospital room with the patient. She was to undergo a double mastectomy, radiation treatments, possibly some chemo and a period of rest. Because the patient was a Christian, I found a worried, yet controlled person. We talked a bit. The conversation was controlled and guided by her. I was actively listening not waiting to "say my say," but hearing her. She said to me over and over, "Pastor, I'm a bit worried but not to the point of being faithless. I cannot explain and can hardly believe this is happening to me. The Lord has brought me 53 years so far and I believe He can carry me through this." It was indeed a glorious privilege and blessing to have shared with her and witness her faith in action. She was terminally ill, and her body was stricken with cancer, yet her spirit was not one of anger or disdain. I found her holding onto her faith in God, amidst her crisis. I prayed for God to have His will and not our will and if our will was in conflict with His will, then, help us accept and conform our will to His will.

I had already spent 20 minutes listening and sharing with the patient. I was ready to make my way to the person I had planned to see when the patient asked if I had CD of a church service with me. I was curious and surprised because no one had ever asked for a CD of the services. Maybe persons wanted to ask, but for some unknown reason they did not ask; however, this patient, from her hospital bed, asked for a CD. Before I could respond, she further remarked, "I want to hear some preaching." I wasn't sure if I had a CD of our services, but I went to my brief case to look. Under the papers and books, God had hidden one CD, just for this moment. The sermon title was *"Shake it Off."* The Bible reference was Acts 28:1-6. I smiled within at the wonderfulness of God, His great love for this woman, whom I had just met. I had not planned to see her that day. As a matter of fact, I didn't even know her. God had her on His mind and planned to help and encourage her through me. His plan was to strengthen her faith and remind her of His faithfulness.

After a few more words of encouragement I walked out of the room, not to ever see her again in this life. I never forget that lesson. I knew we had shared a moment in time where her faith reached out to receive what she needed from God. I, by simply listening, was able to give her what she need at the right time. I considered God's thoughtful orchestration of the events to include, being at the hospital, seeing someone who knew me, hiding the CD in my briefcase and being prepared to minister to the lady. I was there to visit another patient, her daughter recognized me, she boldly sought my assistance, I responded favorably to her request and God hid His word in my briefcase. I am very much an advocate of prepared and purpose driven ministry. I was as encouraged as she was and just as grateful. We entered into a place, she and I, as a small congregation of 2 or 3 to receive the ministry of His presence among us. Nothing ever happens that does not have a deeper and more permanent effect when we are purposeful and understand that ministry is deliberate, especially to the terminally ill.

I now operate with experience, making sure there is a CD in my briefcase at all times because I never know when the occasion will present itself to minister the preached word. It is not pride; it is being prepared to bring the message of hope and life to the home or hospital bound. I now take a deliberate action to insure I have whatever is needed to meet the needs of the terminally ill. Like an experienced traveler, I pack for the trip. I learned again, as I did with the buying of my car (mentioned in a previous chapter), that God has purpose in everything we do. The terminal illness is not outside His purposeful work in and through us. It is not enough to simply be present but to also be prepared for the needs that are all around us. Our assistance to the terminally ill must be deliberate, prepared but not rehearsed. Those who will be involved in this great work must be of a willing and loving spirit and must also be prepared.

This day was a day familiar to the daily exercise regiment which keeps building up endurance and capabilities while adding to what we can already do. To know the different stages of response to terminal illness and to have confidence that the assistance you provided is effective, knowledgeable and necessary; it is God sent and therefore it is essential. Training, preparing, being sensitive and confident in helping the terminally ill patient find peace and strength in God to face the everyday challenge of living with a terminal illness requires we maintain readiness fitness.

We measure the success of life by
a different and more permanent
or eternal rule when we have the
inspired Word of God in us and
when our lives are faith infused.

Chapter 17

THE TRUTH THAT REVIVES US

*T*erminal illness is the road less traveled. For many persons who are ill, inspiration can be found in the preaching of God's word. Persons who are experiencing a terminal illness will need to be inspired regardless of their personal convictions. In medical terminology they require *resuscitation for life to continue.* Inspiration is needed when all the collected medical facts have predicted death is near, life is rapidly slipping away and the body can begin to feel the unwanted trauma and pain. This inspiration has the ability to pull one back from darkness into the light of faith which is quietly working behind the scenes.

John Smith attended the home going service of one of the faithful members of our church. This member was God focused and very much committed to his faith. John Smith was not a member but was related to the family. John Smith was not a believer of God's word and certainly not a church member. He was one who did not fear God and who lived his life according to his own standards. He was 41 years old and had not attended church since his boyhood years. His church attendance on this day was merely out of respect for the passing of a beloved relative. He sat as an onlooker, maybe even a mocker in the services. He listened to the word spoken by the preacher to his family members and loved ones. Whatever feelings John had were hidden behind his mask of duty and distance. John Smith was spiritually lost and his condition was also terminal in another way.

Unknown to me, two weeks prior John Smith had tested positive for HIV, the virus causing the natural defense system of the body to shut down. His condition had reached a level commonly called *"full blown AIDS."* Because John was not a faith filled person and was without a relationship with God, he struggled with coming to church, as well as with and the diagnosis he had received. It was difficult for him to be a part of the home going celebration with a death sentence hanging over his life. After all, what was there to celebrate? His loved one had succumbed to death and now it loomed in his near future. As far as John was concerned, it was the end of the matter, the finality of life. Now here he sat facing his own mortality without any hope for his future.

After the home going service and the burial, we all returned to the church for a traditional fellowship meal. I was in my office resting, relaxing and focusing on the sermon I had not long ago delivered. I was going through a self-inflicting critique for the purpose of doing better the next time and there will always be a next time. In the midst of my self evaluation I heard a knock at my door. I answered it and there, standing at the office door was John Smith. He rather nervously introduced himself to me fumbling over his words. I could see that he was uneasy and was not comfortable or relaxed talking to a minister. In his introduction, he made it clear to me that he had some concerns and asked if I would have time to talk with him. Sensing the frustration, loneliness, fear and the absence of genuine companionship or someone to talk to and share his concerns with, I responded positively to his request.

As I sat listening intently to every word John spoke, this 41 year old man, in an open, impassionate and factual fashion began sharing his story from the beginning of his life to the present. He gave me a thorough history and briefing on who John Smith was, is and wants to be. We spent nearly two and half hours together sharing. I learned that he was HIV positive and that it was through his compromised lifestyle that he believed he became infected. Since finding out this information, two weeks prior, he had cut off all relationships. John had not told anyone of his infection or the prognosis. When his partner asked to come over to his apartment, he told him that he did not want to see him anymore. The partner simply responded, "Okay." John said, "He knew that he was the source of his infection."

Devastated by this medical revelation and having had some education concerning AIDS, John shared with me that he was scared and had been scared for the last two weeks. Even the home going service of his loved one today terrified him. He did not want to face the world or his family and friends being HIV positive. Finally he made the decision to come to church, to leave his house to seek the fellowship of family and to be in the midst of people without divulging his own condition. He also said, "Why not church?" John realized shutting himself off from the world was not good and that he needed to open up. Yet he was still untrusting of what responses he would receive from family and from the church. He felt his secret would somehow be found out and he would be rejected. The last thing John needed was to be ostracized by the whole world he knew.

I later learned that John's reason for being in my office was because of the sermon. "Pastor it was something about your sermon that made me feel deserving, even accepted and simply good on the inside. I felt I was not alone, I felt somehow connected or at the least welcomed." John felt the possibility that somebody cared. He did not feel hopeless or over taken by the reality of death as he heard the eulogy that day. I think he said that "I felt comforted. I felt that maybe there is some hope, some comfort and some life yet left for me. Hearing the Word of God and seeing the words of the Bible come alive, inspired me. I could feel the inspiration that came from the sermon as you preached. I felt better in my mind and even my body for just coming to church. I felt somehow revived."

John lit up my office with hope, his countenance changed the more he talked. The sermon, the preached word, inspired him to look beyond his terminal illness. He was still infected, but now he had hope. He had been affected. He had been inspired. He no longer felt alone, friendless and without companionship. The preached Word of God had given him a handle that would help to address the concerns of his spiritual being. John eventually joined the church. He accepted Christ as his personal Savior and has been a wonderful and caring member. Since becoming a faith filled member, he has personally committed himself to reaching HIV positive persons who may be shutting themselves off from the world and more importantly, shutting themselves off from God. God has a special work for John because he not only heard the word, but responded to the message. John is now GOD POSITIVE.

Preaching to the terminally ill person is inspirational. It comforts and inspires one to look and travel beyond their personal illness and problems. When the future is void and dark, preaching encourages. It is light shining in darkness. When in the whirlwinds of despair, confusion and fear, preaching can still and quiet one's spirit, pushing the patient to the next level where they can enjoy the peace of a breathtaking view even in adversity.

It is a continuation of the life journey, filled with new wonders yet to be experienced. The spoken, preached word lifts the fallen, breathes again revival in a diminished and failing body and mind. It arms and fortifies the weary, giving peace beyond comprehension in the knowing that regardless of what we endure, the faithfulness of God is a sure anchor. This is a medicine that cannot be found in drug stores, supermarkets, pharmaceutical companies, on the shelves of convenience stores or given by street corner druggists. This medicine of inspiration is only found and experienced through what can be labeled the mystery and the hidden blessings and fullness of the preached word.

It goes beyond quoting scriptures from a ready reference to a heartfelt compassion. It is the confidence of a Higher Power who in Himself was and is, in touch with the feeling of our infirmities, our liabilities and our every weaknesses. How can we who say we represent Him put so much distance or misunderstanding as stumbling blocks in the way of others, especially the terminally ill? How can we make the path cluttered with traditions, ignorance and obstacles when we are those called to clear the path and make His way plain and straight? It is through not only preaching or speaking but also the sensitivity, penetrating power of words empowered by our faith that consoles and inspires the terminally ill. God underscores with clarity and simplicity every word filled with the essence of who He is and what He has and will do. To come to Him, the fountain of all healing and the giver of life eternal, to receive without cost, natural and eternal benefits. The preaching of the Word of God is infused with who God is and touches the hearts and minds to bring aid and help us believe what was before...unbelievable.

Terminal illness it is a breathtaking experience of life. **We measure the success of life by a different and more permanent or eternal rule when we have the inspired Word of God in us and when our lives are faith infused**. That faith comes to us in our hearing, through the simplicity of the preached word. It is available today if hearts yield to the message. The walls that have been built up can be dismantled and a doorway opened to life and hope. Yesterday is over, all mistakes can be forgiven and one can receive eternal life and hope that can and will revive. The breath that first quickened can keep one even amidst terminal illness. In the spoken word there is not only hope but healing presence and amazing power. Listen today while it is yet today, while you can hear new life eternal in the spoken Word of God. If one accept the words of faith and allow that word entrance into their living it can work a miracle in the life of the terminally ill.

No terminally ill persons
should fear death.
They do not have to face death
alone nor be tormented.
They should have peace
in knowing death is not the
ultimate end, but merely a
transition into the full
presence of the Lord.

Chapter 18

THE TRUTH THAT CONVERTS AND REASSURES

The significance of calling something by its right name becomes clear especially when you are trying to order a particular item. Have you ever stood at the counter and the name of what you want literally escapes you? You are trying to explain and you say things like, "I want that thing-a-ma-bob, you know the do-hickey that goes on the thing-a-ma-gig with the hook on it." You are trying so hard to sound intelligent when in reality you have simply forgotten the name of the part you need. It is an important part because the vehicle, motor, shelf, window or whatever cannot operate without it. It is the all too important component like the glue that keeps the whole mechanism held together. You know that without the "what-cha-ma- call- it" the whole project or apparatus will not function.

Often what we forget is our greatest help agent. The book of Acts has rightly declared, there is no other name given under the heavens whereby we must be saved, except by the name Jesus. Faith allows us the opportunity to have that name etched in our hearts, minds and being. Through the avenue of preaching we become more familiar with the name and our faith is secured.

Preaching gives clarity and form to both the churched and the un-churched. The hopelessness we experience in the world today can be overcome by the victory of Christ and that is the name we should not forget. Our faith is the essential puzzle piece that makes the whole picture of life come together.

Faith is what we put into our being that will help us outlive the current distresses and endure the illnesses of life. We live forever by faith in His name and He has said *"Whosoever liveth and believeth in me shall never die but shall have everlasting life."* Death is swallowed up in the victory and we become partakers sharing this victory in life and in death. The preached word has the ability to transform and energize our lives if we let it. A faith centered life helps us to make better decisions about what we put in our bodies to better help sustain life.

Thoughtless life styles, horrendous eating habits and poor selection of food are causing more and more persons to be added to the growing number of the terminally ill. We have been so commercialized and indoctrinated into the fast and easy food courts of life that we are thoughtlessly eating and depriving our bodies of the important life sustaining nutrients we need to promote good health. Even our ability to fight off the aggressive attack of terminal illness is weakened by eating habits that do not include vital food components that build and sustain our immune systems. Napoleon Bonaparte, a French military and political leader during the latter stages of the French Revolution said, "An army marches on its stomach," indicating that without the proper diet, victory may well escape us as the army will be too weak to fight over the invaders.

The terminally ill include the young as well as the old. It is almost unbearable to watch a love one endure terminal illness. We are helpless at the bedside as we watch them slowly succumbing to the sickness that will not liberate or allow them to return to good health. The strength that we need to carry on a good fight during the terminal illness can be directly tied to what we eat physically and faithfully. As helpers, caretakers, family members, medical professionals and friends, it is distressing to watch the person carry the load of a terminal illness without faith. The load is so heavy. Without someone to cast the load upon, the patient is left to carry it all alone.

The patient is already hindered by the terminal illness and is left to endure the illness without the necessary name ingredient for continual help. We are reminded by the Apostle Peter to *"Cast our care upon the Lord.* These include the heavy pieces of life, the burdens we are unable or too weak to carry. The "care," the daily responsibility that has overloaded us, is too much for us to carry. We can cast it full force upon the Lord. He is still a burden bearing God who is willing to carry our load. One can call His name in the midst of struggle, for strength and He can reward with victory.

In my interviewing and gathering statistics I have discovered generally one out of five persons who is terminally ill is a Christian. The other four persons are struggling with God absent in their lives. Life is filled with confusion, frustration, physical pain and anguish. Without the presence of FAITH IN GOD, it is impossible to endure. The patient's torment is multiplied ten times when faith is absent from their life. For the persons who are terminally ill and have no genuine relationship with God, life is lived with a constant feeling of failure and hopelessness. Life has become unstable, unbearable and they no longer look forward to the rising of the sun and the beauty of a full moon on a clear autumn night. One can no longer hope or see beauty, only the pain and aloneness. How torturous it is to see a terminally ill person moving toward death who does not know God as a help and a reinforcement of life.

Children are often afraid of the dark because it represents the unknown. Fear of the unknown takes control of the mind, the soul and the spirit. Sometimes the best way to cure the fear is simply to turn on the light because with the light on they can see they have nothing to fear. Often they simply need Daddy to come into the room and assure their hearts that He will not allow anything to harm them. He demonstrates that he has power over any invader and will be with them throughout the night. We come into the room of the terminally ill to turn the light on and reassure them that nothing is hiding under the bed or anywhere else that can harm them. We bring the presence of the Father into the sick room to remind them that He is always present and nothing can harm or defeat them. They are protected; they are under the shadow of the wings of the Almighty and they are safe and saved.

The terminally ill patient who sees himself alone and outside of the reach of forgiveness has no consolation available. It seems as if they have not reached a point where even God can get in. This hopelessness is an aloneness of soul and mind, where the patient feels isolated without any internal strength. It seems as though one is caught up in a frenzy that will not release his soul. Many times I have experienced this internal hopelessness and weariness in my interviewing of terminally ill patients. They are overtaken in panic and hopelessness has possessed their every waking moment and it does not afford them rest. They are staring into a great nothingness trying to make sense out of what is senseless to them. They continue to rehearse over and over the failures of the past and cannot receive what hasn't been offered. Can you imagine finding an almost dying and thirsty man in the desert and you have water yet you are not sure if it is the right time to offer him a drink?

I had made several visits to a young man about 33 years old. He was a patient transferred to a local hospice from the hospital. His state of mind was hostile and he was hopelessly angry. He was angry with the world; he hated the doctors and other medical professionals. Can you imagine hating the very people entrusted with your care? I found that despite his negative attitude and his lack of patience with health care workers, he allowed me to have conversations with him. He requested that I not read the Bible or pray with or for him. However, he wanted me to answer seemingly random, irrelevant, questions about God. His questions appeared to be specifically designed to trap me in contradictions. The Lord was my helper and gave me the grace to answer each question without the use of the Bible to bring faith into a reasonable and understandable way to him, despite the limits he gave me.

Although he would not allow me to pray for him or read scriptures, I believe, in a strange way, he was able to see that what he secretly hoped for was a relationship with God. He knew very little about the God and his negative opinions about God were lacking knowledge. His doctors and nurses began to notice a slight, but positive change in him as days went by. The last days of his life were most miserable for him. He was still a man who resisted faith. He resisted the Lord as his personal Savior. He came close to the comprehending of God but would not allow himself to be engulfed in it to believe in God. He was almost persuaded but could not get past the anger that continued to eat up his ability and his strength to resist the illness.

His mother would visit from Virginia often. She stated that when he became ill, he was so depressed that he almost destroyed her home in a rage. The mother was not a Christian and she appeared to blame herself for her son's attitude about his unexpected death encounter. Without faith he approached death without any hope and that was very agonizing. He struggled in his aloneness for three nights; he was without rest or peace. This patient had no spiritual comfort, no spiritual peace or assurance of the continuation of life. Even though the nurses gave him high doses of medications to ease the pain, he could not rest. In his final moments as I entered his room, watching the nurse search for his pulse, I walked over to his bedside. His eyes were still open. His face expressed he had not peacefully relinquished life but was fearfully fighting until the very end. His death was void of hope.

No terminally ill persons should fear death. They do not have to face death alone nor be tormented. They should have peace in knowing death is not the ultimate end, but merely a transition into

the full presence of the Lord. With such a high percentage of persons who are not living in faith and who have not surrendered to the Lord's will, we must find ways to expose them to the gospel so conversation can take place. We must be patient and persistent as it becomes obligatory for us to share faith and the plan of Salvation so they can experience a God of peace. I sincerely believe if the above referenced patient, who died not knowing the Lord, had lived a bit longer, he would have accepted the Lord. He chose to fight the wrong battle, forfeiting the only true help available. With all the strength he had left, he fought his Helper.

The person who is terminally ill can receive hope and be in faith through the preached gospel as long as they can be reached. The scriptures give witness to this fact. Jesus Christ, while dying on Calvary's cross, was asked by one thief, "If you're the Son of God, save yourself and save us." This thief did not believe Jesus was the Christ; he jeered and ridiculed him. The other thief, on the other side of the cross had a much clearer view and a different request. He said, "Master, when you come into thy kingdom, remember me." The record indicates Jesus lifted up a hung down head, turned painfully to that thief, who lived against both the law of heaven and of earth and said, "This day, you will be with me in paradise." Salvation was extended to that thief in his last moments as he moved toward death. Though he was dying, he was saved because he asked for Salvation and because Jesus saves and He can save in a dying moment.

A person's last days can be their best days. Physically that may be difficult; however, spiritually it can be accomplished. We all have a dust date, a life expiration date. It is a date that cannot be canceled or postponed. It is a date that can't be delayed. It is a date that already has been recorded in the divine datebook of God. Therefore, every person should have a genuine relationship with the one who knows our expiration date. Being terminally ill is a heavy load to bear, but with God, the load is both bearable and sharable. Absolutely no terminally ill patient should die without the opportunity of hearing the gospel of Jesus Christ. We must prepare ministry that can serve until the opportunity presents itself to introduce Salvation.

I have witnessed persons who were terminally ill, bodies stricken with cancer, yet from their sick beds gave witness to God's goodness and His forever keeping power. Others had voices that could only speak in whispers, but in a raspy whisper, they magnified the Lord their keeper. During the last few days of her life, one patient said to me, "If He blesses me, it will be fine. If He heals my body it will be fine. But if does not heal my body, it will still be fine. I know that either way, whether now or later, on this side or on the other, He is still mine." Within a week, I was informed that she moved forward into life renewed and a peaceful smile could be seen on her face.

Christians are not exempt from terminal illness. Yet we can face death with assurance in knowing there is no sting or victory hanging over our heads in death. Christians know the final resting place is not the grave, which is limited, but it is in the limitless presence of the Lord. The terminally ill person who has surrendered to the will of God can face death fearlessly. What a wonderful testimony to receive His blessings when physical life is running out.

Often it is not until the upset,
the tragic event or the
uncontrollable and unreasonable
situation happens, faith will
emerge to strengthen and
provide a great calm.

Chapter 19

PREACHING IS PREPARATION

$\mathcal{A}$ ll the good works, companionship and assistance we can provide the terminally ill will not provide faith and assurance of the afterlife. Although we can help the patient adjust, preaching allows the patient to prepare for physical death. This preparation enables the patient to accept the physical death based upon their understanding of God at work in their present and future living. Death is not seen as the end of all existence. Rather it is seen as a transition to being with God for all eternity. Now with that being said, preaching with passion, prose and persuasion is important. Nothing happens if one is unable to preach with power and conviction. That power has the ability to transform lives and bring understanding and hope into every situation of life. Paul states in Timothy 1:11-12 that he is appointed to be a preacher void of shame as he knows in whom he believes and is thoroughly persuaded of God's ability to keep and maintain even in adversity what he has committed everything unto Him until the very end.

As previously mentioned, on Tuesday January 12, 2010, a 7.0 earthquake hit Haiti. The catastrophic results were seen worldwide as the worst earthquake in this region in 200 years. The people of Haiti had their lives interrupted and devastated by a sudden event that could not be controlled. In traveling there to assess the damage and participate in the relief effort, the chaos hindered much of the immediate relief actions. As I looked at familiar places I had visited many times, it was amazing to see chaos in one area and another area seemingly undisturbed, almost tranquil. The faith of the people remained intact even amidst the chaos and destruction. It was an amazing testimony to the ability of faith to prevail in the midst of sudden devastating situations. When life was upset, interrupted by the sudden event of a natural catastrophe, faith, hope and the ability to endure surfaced. **Often it is not until the upset, the tragic event or the uncontrollable and unreasonable situation happens, faith will emerge to strengthen and provide a great calm.**

As a pastor and one who assists in humanitarian efforts, I have seen great poverty and lack, yet I have also found a people open and receptive to the faithful teaching and preaching of the gospel. This is been evidenced even in remote areas of Haiti, Cuba and Kenya. The power of the Word of God infuses and transforms lives with hope and assures persons of recovery that brings peace often during great unrest. The faithful declaration and the subsequent results of preaching is evidenced by the hope and conviction of the people demonstrated in their daily lives of recovery and perseverance. Traveling as a member of the recovery team I witnessed firsthand the receptivity of the people to not only hear, but receive the engrafted word of faith that has the ability to save and transform lives. I have been both humbled by the understanding and the results of the impact of the power of the preached word. I have been afforded the opportunity to participate in the ushering in of hope during devastating and traumatic events. I have come to understand the power of the Word of God to sustain, prepare, transform and comfort in the midst of adversity and life reversals.

God's primary means of transmitting information and infusing hope to the masses is through men and women who dare to preach the hope of the gospel as careful and concerned stewards, entrusted to convey this life-changing information. Physical recovery happens over time with planning, government assistance and contingency plans, but the hope and faith needed for people to live in and through tragedies can happen immediately. Help, hope and peace are available the moment they believe. Lives are being impacted by truth and are being immediately strengthened within by faith. Lives are literally held in the balance. When one considers the importance of the message of faith that person becomes more careful and prayerful to receive the messages with the understanding that this is enormously helpful.

Preaching goes forth with strong convictions declaring truth and peace in the midst of a raging battle between terminal illness and life. In accepting and going forward, preaching becomes the trumpet of hope or the Calvary rushing to the battle at the right time with help to overcome.

It is of necessity that we preach the gospel; we are ordered and ordained to deliver the living, breathing, unchanging Word of God with the power of persuasion. Paul declares in Romans 1:16; "I am not ashamed of the gospel because it is the power of God." Think about that one for a moment. We preach with the power of God. It is the work and word of preparation, just as Jesus spoke to His disciples, assuring them that *He goes to prepare a place for them. As He goes to prepare the place for them, He will return and receive them to Himself.* He assures them that where He is they will be also. If Jesus prepares for His disciples, He also prepares for us. As He prepared them He also prepares us. To the terminally ill persons, with debilitating diseases, the assurance of a prepared place also prepares them for physical death.

The thief who was being put to death received Salvation on the spot. Right there on the cross, while being executed, he received paradise and the eternal presence and peace of the Master. He faced a grueling and agonizing death assured of a joy filled eternity. He was indeed prepared for death since he was in the midst of his sentence being executed, but instead eternal life was given. In fact, he was so prepared for death, that death was no longer feared. Preaching allows the terminally ill patient to know and experience this hope and assurance in the now of their suffering and pain. It has the life extension hope that is able to transform the mind from the penetrating pain to an eternal rest with the comfort of the presence and promise of God.

The thief did not have the opportunity to physically leave the cross. He did not travel to an oasis in the Virgin Islands, but right there, spiritually, Jesus transformed his mind and gave him a life extension. The thief experienced paradise in the middle of human destruction, human degradation and a body tortured by pain. He acknowledged the author of His faith and simply asked to be remembered. When we consider being "remembered," this thief was asking Christ to keep His mind filled with him. In other words he asked Jesus not to forget him and to keep him connected with Him in His kingdom transition. He understood he wanted more than just death. He believed in the Lordship of Christ and His kingdom. He accepted the current cross and impending death would not be the end of Him. This is the power of the preaching of the cross of Christ. It is life in the midst of what is defined as death. It is the preaching of the eternal kingdom of God.

I was asked by the family of a cancer patient to visit and to pray for the patient. The patient was in severe uncontrollable pain. The medication, at that point, was useless. As I entered the room, I noticed the doctor examining the patient. The doctor could clearly see that I was clergy and he shared with me that he doubted seriously if the patient would live through the night. (Remember that we previously discussed that the last sense to leave is hearing?) My compassion and concern as a pastor was aroused by the *matter of fact* manner in which the information was shared. Yet, I noticed the patient could hear our conversation, but was not bothered by the information. The patient's lack of response grabbed my attention and I came closer to her to both reassure her and to understand her apparent peace.

I could see that there was a peaceful spirit and a spirit of assurance in knowing that God had already prepared the patient for this time. The patient was in much pain, but the patient was at peace. This paradoxical life situation not only intrigued me, but again, I knew another small voice was speaking telling me that pain and peace can coexist and not clash. The patient could not lie still because of the pain and yet, the patient could speak with great assurance that God still has the last word, above and beyond earthly doctors. She was living in an unexplainable peace and power of God that surpasses our ability to understand or articulate it. We

This woman of faith and I communed in prayer together..

After the doctor left the room and it was just the two
of us, along with the presence of the Lord, I said to the
patient, "To be with you and to witness a faith still
strong and holding on to God in decreasing minutes is
a blessing for me. What keeps you? I know it is more
than just believing in God. There are many who believe
but still find they are unprepared for the final day. They
are still living in fear, failure and not in faith." With a
whisper of a voice that was being tried by the pain, she
endured and she helped me to understand a greater
truth. She said, "The Word of God keeps me on the
track. I cannot read it now but the words are written in
my heart. Sermons I have heard in my lifetime, I still
have in my heart. I am holding on to the words, the
memories of the preached word. God promised never to
leave me, His words are, 'Lo, I am with you always, even
to the end of time.'" The frail and dying lady continued.
With her body reduced to skin and bone, with precious
energy she said, "I once heard a sermon preached entitled *An Ever Present God*."

This amazing woman who was a cancer patient was
holding on to the words of God as she remembered
them. She chose to bring them again to her still conscious mind while going through the valley and shadow
of death. They were hidden in the deep recesses of her

heart as seeds that continued to grow and were accessible to her in her time of need. She would not entertain
unbelief or give up in adversity because the Word of God
in her was yet active and alive, it would not die. She held
on to life even as physical death quickly approached.
Preaching is preparation for the days that come so often
unexpectedly and with a sudden, deadly impact. I often
remind our membership; if you haven't experienced adversity or your faith hasn't been challenged lately, just
keep on living. This is what this precious woman continued to do even in the midst of approaching death; she
was determined by the Word of God, to keep on living.
She was having her own revival of the Word of God. She
recalled Jesus being tempted in the wilderness; "man
does not live by bread alone but by every word proceeding from the mouth or Word of God."

Faith prepares us for the ultimate appointment we
all have with death. The hearing of the Word of God
given by the preacher can be stored and hidden in our
hearts to be accessed as a sweet fruit of courage in the
times of our greatest need. We limit ourselves when we
limit our exposure to the faith filled Word of God. One
of the evidences of the end of time is the fact that men
will not endure sound doctrine, which is the preaching
of the Word of God. If we keep living, the time will come
when we will need the assurance of the word we have
heard *to walk by faith and not by sight.* We will walk re-

gardless of the report of the medical authorities and we will run and not become weary even though physically confined to our beds.

To get through the obstacle course of life so often set to destroy and discourage us, we can rely upon the preaching of the Word of God to prepare and arm us. We can navigate through the thorny places of life only by the assurance it brings to still save and deliver. Preaching gives hope by letting us know that death is merely a comma, not a period and life after death is both a promise and a reward. This articulation and affirmation of faith will support us and reassure us when traveling through pain and the impending loss of the life. Assurance brings hope and peace midst the warfare of terminal illness. Words of faith will penetrate, support and uphold us when the iron grip of sickness comes as a tormenter to tell us we are alone and without God's assistance. Faith becomes the anchor on our ship that will steady us with confidence in the storm of life.

As I interview and minister to many terminally ill patients, I know that faith filled words provide hope beyond the medical treatment. Every piece of knowledge we have has its limits; we only know in part. When medical professionals reach the extent of their abilities, we do not have to lose heart and become hopeless or faithless. Teaching is a gift God has given to the church and it is profitable for maturing and yet, teaching can often become a debate where information is being challenged. The terminally ill patient doesn't have the time and often the ability to be taught. Teachers will sometimes inject their opinions or interpretations of a particular doctrine in the process of developing their lesson. Teaching has its appropriate place and meets the need that it was designed to meet. However, at the end of the road, the long tedious journey, the words we really want to hear affirmed is, we have arrived at our "hoped for" destination.

Preaching is the authoritative speaking of God into the lives of His people for the purpose of giving and sustaining life in them. It is the respirator that allows the initial breath they were given in the garden to continue beyond the grave. In the gospel of John (the first chapter) we are reminded that the Word was life and that life became light that destroyed the power of darkness forever. When we are walking through valleys and shadows of death we shall not fear because we are assured by His word of His continual presence with us. The Word of God reminds us that faith has come by His word that we may have life eternally and abundantly. God so loved the world that He gave His Son. We were given an eternal life sentence and that extension of life is filled with wonder and joy inexpressible. This is the word, the declaration that not only sustains us but gives us life from the moment we first heard and believed it throughout our eternal existence. The life of God in us will never die.

This is the truth of the gospel we preach.

Finally, it is through preaching that the terminally ill patient is made ready, fortified and prepared to move from a temporary life to an eternal life. Death has lost any dominion or power over the patient. They are the living victory, the faith that overcomes the principles and teachings of the world through the word alive in them. Faith has been declared and men not only hear it but they receive its victory. By the word, they became over-comers, more than conquerors and victors in the battle for life. For the patient, many times the preacher is God's messenger and the listener receives the words they declare as coming directly from God to them. It is a personal invite to the eternal presence of God. The authority of the sermon becomes the authority, the reaching of God. The Word is the new medicine unknown by medical professionals for treatment of the conditions of life for those who will surrender, accept and believe in God. We are reminded in Romans chapter 10 that *we are unable to believe what we haven't heard and we cannot hear unless God sends us a preacher.* The preacher cannot preach unless he or she has been assigned and sent by God for the purpose of preaching the life extending gospel which is new life to the hearer.

When one considers the importance of the mission given to declare the uncompromised gospel, one will, with sobriety and humility, preach faith and assurance of life eternal through faith in God. The eternal lives of men and women are held in the balance as persons armed with the Word of God are sent to prepare and declare life in the midst of death and dying. We are those commissioned to go into the world to increase and confirm the kingdom of God. As preachers, we are to be known by those who are bearing crosses in life and death, as carriers of the hope of God. How can they believe if they have not heard? We must be ever careful and prayerful of what we are saying. Lives depend upon the Word of God. Effective ministry is prepared ministry. It requires us to be partakers of the hope and faith we preach, being assured of the authenticity of the word of life we release.

The Word we have been given and are prepared to share also prepares the listener to fight the good and the torrential fight of faith. This fight of faith overcomes the terror and adversary called death and gives us a daily victory over fear, failure and the grave. The Word we declare and share can be stored, is preserved in the hearts of the hearers and will come to life and fight for them against every opposing adversary. The terminally ill patient requires the Word of God preached not to them but received in them. As the storehouse of the Word of God is activated in them, it will arise in the battle for life to give them the power and assurance they need to defeat death, knowing death has no territorial rights over them. The terminally ill patient, like the woman with cancer, can live with pain and still be worry free. The people in Haiti buried under the rubble of stones were heard singing songs of praise and giving testimony of a fearless faith. Their faith kept them alive, literally. In the Kenyan slums and squatter camps, I found shacks swept clean and smiling faces greeting us at the doorways. This was because the Word of God was preached and stored in them for the day when it is most needed. This word gives them victory and deliverance in the crisis of life today.

Knowledge is the accumulation of
the facts and wisdom answers
the questions of how,
when, where and why.

Chapter 20

A LABOR OF LOVE

I am one who believes in the power of prayer. I am guilty of praying for persons I love, persons who I know and for persons whose names have been given to me. I participate in a weekly prayer effort that is designed to strengthen one's commitment to prayer. I will sometimes get up early to attend a 6:00a.m. to 7:00a.m. prayer session. I encourage persons to pray and I personally have committed to consistent daily prayer. I understand that prayer is a foundational principle for pleasing God. God wants to hear from us daily because we are His children. He is a caring father. Prayer is the glue that cements us together as we gather in church for prayer during the week, at noonday worship, evenings worship and on Sundays. On Sunday morning I am there, most of the time holding hands with the choir, praying as we prepare for worship. It is vitally important that we demonstrate what we teach. Everything that we are taught in the Word of God has great meaning for our lives. Instruction can only take us so far; it is limited. But actions are reproductive, they help us form habits good and unfortunately, sometimes bad ones. As a family, my wife and I pray together, for partnership in marriage, for one another, for good health, for our children and for the effectiveness of the work of the ministry. We pray for finances, the administration of the church, outreach and growth in ministry and for excellence in the work God has given us. I cannot stress enough the power and purpose of prayer in all that we do. Prayer is essential for direction, consecration, unity of purpose, empowerment, protection and the ability to do the work of ministry. Life is often tedious in that it can become repetitious and all results are not immediate or measurable. The work of ministry is nonstop. Without prayer we become faint, weary and impatient and we can lose the ability to minister in an effective and cohesive manner. Just like your car requires that you stop regularly at the gas station for fuel, prayer gives us fuel and is essential for the work of the ministry. The ministry to the terminally ill begins and continues in prayer. It is the bulwark, the support of the work to be done. As a pastor and as an organizer I am the model that demonstrates the importance of God centered and empowered ministry to the terminally ill and their families. Whatever you plan to do, it should begin, be directed, formatted, empowered and covered in prayer.

It is important not to begin ministry without a map, without direction and protection. Zeal is great; we need people full of the desire and energy to do the work. However, assistance to the terminally ill is demanding, requiring creative energy in order to be productive. We need both, understanding and wisdom to apply all our knowledge correctly and sensitively. **Knowledge is the accumulation of the facts and wisdom answers the questions of how, when, where and why.** Wisdom is vital. As James 1:12 aptly reminds us, wisdom comes from God. It is vital as leaders and participants to understand the weight and value of the work we undertake to the terminally ill. This is another area in the vineyard of God to be harvested. The workers must be prepared and made ready. As leaders we are responsible for preparing and assisting those who will work with the terminally ill and we must, ourselves, be familiar with the needs of the patient and those who will do the actual work of ministry.

As you begin to format the ministry, diversity is an essential part of this effort for effectiveness. You need different temperaments because they bring a blend of thought, creativity and perceptions. You want the quiet reserved person and you want *the sand that irritates until a pearl is produced* type person. Both types are essential for the work being done. They are the *why and how people* who force change or validation of the current methodology being used. You need young people, older people, men and women. In other words, no one is excluded but everyone must be prepared. As you may notice, I continually use the terminology of preparation.

Compare ministry preparation to a good meal; it should be appetizing, nutritional, balanced, palatable, served at the right temperature and at the right time. Everything that goes along with that good meal should enhance it, bring out its flavor and not take away from it. We have many people who are willing to do ministry. They say yes but they are waiting for leadership to prepare, equip and encourage them in the work they are called and waiting to do. Planning, preparation, patience and willingness are prerequisites to effective assistance to the terminally ill.

I have been compelled to establish effective ministry to the terminally ill. It began in the same way as this book began, by expanding the scope of how one views the terminally ill. It is very important to know as much as possible about the terminally ill patient to insure the best results. What may appear to be clinical information to some helps in understanding the nature and the responses one will have to accept the announcement and progression of terminal illness. Just as a mechanic cannot properly service a machine void of knowledge of the machine and the nature of the problem, so it is with a person who is to effectively care for the terminally ill. Another word for stages is the word responses. If responses are considered and expected, they can also be better understood. Workers in this area of helps require specific knowledge and skills to meet the needs of the patient and family. Just as the mechanic, in order to properly service the equipment and restore it, one will need to grasp the entire picture from start to finish. So it is with the great work of providing a "Labor of Love" for the terminally ill.

In the preceding chapters I have earnestly exposed and given relevant concerns in a compassionate manner to provide understanding to aid in relating to terminal illness. There are at least two interpretations of terminally illness: a physical perspective and a spiritual perspective. A terminal illness can be viewed as a fact of life or a curse. It all depends on perspective and understanding. In the same manner a blessing is often difficult to define, especially when persons are in constant pain and suffering. Medicine is not able to alleviate the physical torment; death appears eminent. With a better understanding of the responses and a plan to effectively help the terminally ill patient, we can be in a position to assist, care with concern and be a companion and comfort in this time of illness. Death is in reality often the end of the known and the entering into the unknown.

Persons who are rigid in their approach to the Bible can view terminal illness only in a limited structure that may include being a curse from God. It can be projected by some who believe when one is sick or have a terminal illness it is because of sin and due to a lack of faith in God. Their view becomes the cursed view and it is hopelessness and failure that they unintentionally provide. In this view the curse is a weight that cannot be lifted; it is God ordained in this limited perspective of terminal illness. The patient believes that they are not only suffering physically, but they are suffering because God is angry at them and is punishing them. They have no recourse, no appeal or hope. How do you appease an angry and vindictive God who is punishing you because of your past actions? How do you obtain mercy or help from an angry God? There are consequences of actions if you cross the street against the light. Cars may not stop. If you jump off a building, the law of gravity will take effect. As we have previously discussed, this view is narrow and does not lead the terminally ill patient to the hope of God and any hope of recovery or remission.

Terminal illnesses can be a blessing based on one's belief in God. Through faith, we believe that God can bless in every situation. He can make Himself known even in the midst of sickness and impending death. God can change situations from darkness to bright sunshine (miracles are for today and should not be discounted). God can also bring peace in difficult circumstances without changing the reality of the condition. That too is a miracle. In other words, even if a patient doesn't recover from the illness they can still have peace and the hope of God within. They can enjoy the continual grace of God in their lives and a *peace that surpasses all un-*

derstanding. They can enjoy the confidence of salvation and eternal life even in the midst of the terminal illness. And, they can share hope with those they love and experience unusual comfort.

As we look at the steps necessary for establishing and maintaining, effective and continual ministry or support for the terminally ill, we begin in prayer and then move to preparation.

Step one: Creating the environment, preparing the ground work

To prepare and insure acceptable and effective ministry designed to support persons who are terminally ill, education must take place within the group of workers, especially among those who evidence a specific calling for this ministry. A designed format that creates avenues by which knowledge is expanded with awareness, understanding and compassion for the plight of the terminally ill person is essential. Education is not to be feared or dreaded, nor thought of as unspiritual. Education is essential in our understanding of terminal illness and the many responses and views that can hinder the terminally ill from having a God perspective during this time. It is through education, and helpers will give genuine hope for terminally ill persons. It is in this world that we ourselves and the terminally ill are able to live their lives fully, as lights and serve as beacons of hope, especially when darkness and despair terrorize those who do not know the hope and faith of God. Education must be tempered by genuine compassion and a serving heart.

We can accomplish this goal of creating the environment and preparing the ground work in a variety of ways. The components of this phase of the ministry include:

A. Teaching: Planting the seed

- Teaching can inform, expand, direct and provide a compassionate view and appreciation for ministry and support to the terminally ill.

- The Bible is filled with examples and teachings related to Christians loving and caring for one another. We are repeatedly and continually throughout the Bible admonished and instructed to love, care, forgive, support and fellowship with one another. The strong should support and help the weak.

- Having a passion to support terminally ill persons is the seed and a teaching ministry in the watering. A teaching thrust supports, undergirds and provides continual and necessary information to those involved in ministry encouragement and information. It also provides effective teaching within the church to include a multiplicity of resources for utilization as essential tools to equip and transform volunteers into effective ministry workers.

B. The ministry can have an Introductory Orientation workshop

- Awareness is a key to effectiveness and enlistment for the work of ministry. How often do we hear people say, "I know God has called me to do something, but I don't know exactly what it is?" We lead people to Christ and disciple them, yet we expect they should just go to work in the kingdom unprepared, uninformed and untrained. Without knowing where the needs are those who could or would do the work are unaware to the needed areas of work.

- An effective Christian Education Department is in partnership with the pastor in preparing workshops, gathering information, preparing presentations so ministry leaders and participants become aware of the need for ministry to the terminally ill.

- In an awareness workshop information, both biblical and practical, is presented to help format and provide a consistent and continual base of availability of information and help.

- The atmosphere of the workshop is a "can do" approach moving from "the dismal, without hope prognosis" to the "can do" attitude of ministry to the terminally ill.

- In the workshop basic definitions explaining the different perspectives of terminal illness can be examined.

- The workshop should include medical professionals and ministers who have experience and who focus on the needs of the terminally ill. This component provides the basic background information and the foundation for the development of the skills and sensitivity needed to provide a meaningful ministry to the terminally ill patient.

C. Field Trips to a facility for the terminally ill

- To bring awareness to the methods currently being used by mainstream medical professionals and to be introduced to existing organizations who are committed to the terminal ill is essential.

- Help to evaluate the missing components relevant for meaningful care and how we can cooperate and extend ministry to the terminally ill through various types of medical and palliative care is essential.

- Help to view the various stages and limitations of terminal illness and to reinforce the need for effective and sensitive ministry.

- The field trips also help to prepare the ministry

worker for the diverse aspects of attitudes and responses to the terminal illness of the patient, family and medical professionals.

- Post field trips allows for a genuine comparison to prepare for the effective support to the terminally ill. We compare what appears to be working and what can be interjected for the benefit of the terminally ill patient and their families. This coming together allows for mapping out a strategy and to begin the additional training needed for sensitivity, biblical perspective and prayer for the terminally ill and the ministry we are to provide.

D. Team Work and Corporate interaction is the Ministry approach

- In this aspect of preparation and readiness of ministry, the entire ministry is put on active communication alert.
- The evangelistic ministry is looking for opportunities to utilize and provide information to the "Ministry of Presence" people they have been in contact with that may need ministry.
- The missions department is providing names of families who are aware of persons who may need the "Ministry of Presence."
- The pastoral, ministerial and deacons ministry is also looking for opportunities to put the "Ministry

of Presence" to work among the membership and the families of the membership.

- The church office is providing updated membership information to include terminal illness to the ministry.
- The Christian Education team is providing updated ministry materials to include additional training, workshops, encouragement bulletins and any new resource information to include local hospice updates, new facility openings or closings, along with some possible seminars that can enhance the ministry work.

Christian ministry is a challenging vocation that requires a holistic preparation of a person. If you have been called to Christian ministry you probably already feel some of the weight of the task. Follow these steps to become more prepared for what God has called you to do.

Focus on your spiritual development:

Christian ministry is grueling and nonstop. It can tax your spiritual life and you will need to be refilled. Regular church attendance and Bible study are areas where you can be built up to endure the rigors of ministry. To forsake assembling together is to limit your own effectiveness. You will be exposed to deaths, wrestle with tragedies, face persons who are bitter and deal with internal conflicts when you participate in ministry to the terminally ill. You must be continually built up in the faith. Like Joshua, you must be very courageous and confident in knowing God is with you in everything. We cannot, in confidence, present a God who is Lord over the affairs of men, in living and dying, if we have a part time relationship or an *off and on* relationship with Him. It is essential that we are thoroughly persuaded before we can attempt to persuade anyone else.

As a result, you will need a strong, vibrant and continual faith keeping you on target and focused. You need to keep yourself refreshed, not being legalistic or overly traditional about spiritual disciplines, as they will have the opposite effect of your intention. Ministry serves, it undergirds, it covers and it's there to recover others. Ministry is the healing balm of reconciliation and restoration. Spending time in prayer and meditating on scriptures, in a pattern that fits your life, is very important. Remember, just because you are involved and committed to ministry to the terminally ill doesn't mean your own life pauses. Developing a regular and a spontaneous prayer life helps you and gives you the opportunity to cast your every care upon the Lord.

Work on developing your emotional world

After prayerfully making a decision to work in the ministry to the terminally ill, the next step is to make sure that you are prepared. Scripture tells us that *my people are destroyed for lack of knowledge and vision.* This lets us know that while vision is important in the scheme of things, it is also important to have the education and training, the readiness to work in ministry with both knowledge and the wisdom of application. Some ministry opportunities take months while others may take years and require additional education and mentorship. Mentorship is an important part of the process; it affords one the opportunity for Godly advice, prayer support and genuine encouragement. People can be attached to a ministry and never hear a personal word of encouragement. They come Sunday after Sunday, listening to the messages to return to their homes without any personalization or genuine fellowship validating them as important part of the Christian community and in relationship with other believers. Effective ministry connects and bridges the gaps between Sundays. It is dependable and available when needs arise. In ministry we can be certain that the need will arise. The other part of readiness is the continual educational process, the on the job training or internship experience. Internship gives valuable experience but it also lets people know that you are willing to follow through, provide leadership and ministry that is beyond words. It is also present to address the needs of their lives. Everyone will follow through when things are going well.

But God wants to know are you still trusting Him when things are falling apart on the outside.

Building a Support Team:

Confronting the attitudes of, "it is easier for me to just do it myself" or the "I can do it alone" prideful ministry approach causes ministry to be micro and ineffective. I am confident Jesus didn't need the disciples to get the immediate work of reconciliation done. Yet, for the effectiveness and continuation of the work, He invested time, instructions, fellowship, encouragement and often participated in personal one on ones with the disciples. He took them to the mountaintop, across a storm tossed sea, sent them on reconnaissance and they traveled together. Who were these disciples ordinary men who would continue the work and reach masses of people with the ministry of reconciliation? He first delivered to them and then demonstrated. They were not just sitting in a classroom learning but they were often called upon to serve, to tirelessly row in storms, to prepare for the mission, to take the message and trust Him with the results. Behind all good and stable ministries is a team of people willing to assist, encourage and pray for the ministry. These are important people. Building a support team is a necessary step that will take time to build. The larger the number of your prayer partners, the larger your outreach will be. The more support you have, the more effective the work of ministry becomes. Prayer is the place where the battle begins because ministry will be resisted and prayer is the weapon for Spiritual warfare. Your prayer support team is important. Prayer serves as foundation for all that we do. Your team, like your church, is made up of many members who though diversity of gifts and abilities, add to the overall effectiveness of the ministry. This becomes our *Labor of Love*.

EPILOGUE

*I*n the book of Genesis, God told both Adam and Eve, *not to touch nor eat of the tree in the midst of the Garden, for in the day that you eat you will surely die.* God gave them other trees to eat of but the tree in the midst, God gave them clear instructions to stay away. He said to them *the day you eat of that tree you will surely die.*

Adam and Eve were not able to fully understand the weight and the severity of God's clear and unusual directive, so they found themselves disobeying what God Had told them. Their disobedience opened the door for some consequences that they were not prepared to embrace, such things as sickness and physical human decay. Prior to their disobedience there were no sickness, there were no human physical limitations and man lived in a diseased free environment; everything was good.

Adam and Eve disobeyed God and the relationship between humanity and divinity was breeched. God, in His amazing grace and love for humanity, restores the relationship through His son Jesus Christ. Humanity was afforded a relationship with the Father again. As Paul puts it, "*by one man sin entered into the world and by one man we were restored to the father."* Thank God for Jesus, the one who made things right with us and with the Father.

Although humanity has been forgiven and things are good between God and those who have accepted the Jesus Christ as savior, the consequences for the original disobedience remains. *"In the day that you eat of this tree you will surely die"* are the words of God to humanity. We are all on the tract of terminal illness. Everyday our bodies are reminding us that it will not last forever. As we age we find ourselves more vulnerable to diseases and sicknesses. Some infirmities we can manage with proper diet, exercise and medication and other infections are beyond our control and understanding.

Terminal illness cannot be avoided but we can understand it and we can get a handle on it to be able to experience some quality of life at the end of life's journey. The hope that we have is that God is still in control and He knows how much we can bear and he can grant us peace in our final moments. Jesus said to His disciples one day, *"I am the resurrection and the life, he who believes in Me, though he is dead, shall live again and whoever lives and believes in me shall never die but shall have everlasting life."* Each day is another precious opportunity to live life to the best of your God given potential because life on this side is like a vapor with a brief duration.

Ecca 12:1-4

1   Remember now your Creator in the days of your youth, before the difficult days come and the years draw near when you say, "I have no pleasure in them":

2   While the sun and the light, the moon and the stars, are not darkened and the clouds do not return after the rain;

3   In the day when the keepers of the house tremble and the strong men bow down; when the grinders cease because they are few and those that look through the windows grow dim;

4   When the doors are shut in the streets and the sound of grinding is low; when one rises up at the sound of a bird and all the daughters of music are brought low.

5   Also they are afraid of height and of terrors in the way; when the almond tree blossoms, the grasshopper is a burden and desire fails. For man goes to his eternal home and the mourners go about the streets.

6   Remember your Creator before the silver cord is loosed or the golden bowl is broken or the pitcher shattered at the fountain or the wheel broken at the well.

7   Then the dust will return to the earth as it was and the spirit will return to God who gave it.

NJAVE

Resources

On Death and Dying, Elizabeth Kubler-Ross

"Meaning, Mortality and Choice: The Social Psychology of Existential Concerns, Phillip R. Shaver, PhD and Mario Mikulincer, PhD

Black Jack Jetty: A Boy's Journey through Grief, Michael A. Carestio

Bereavement in Late Life: Coping Adaptation and Developmental Influences, Robert O. Hansson and Margaret S. Stroebe

ABOUT THE AUTHOR

J.L. Carter has been the devoted and committed Senior Pastor to Ark Church for more than 27 years. Under his leadership Ark Church has experienced many successes in ministry. Ark Church continues to grow and is recognized as an anchor in the East Baltimore, Maryland community where crime, blight, urban flight and substance abuse are significant. Dr. Carter continues to serve the people with excitement that never runs low.

He is a graduate of the Samuel Dewitt Proctor School of Theology, Virginia Union University, Richmond, Virginia. He holds a Masters of Divinity Degree and has received his Doctor of Divinity Degree, United Theological

Seminary, Dayton, Ohio. He successfully completed three year Certificate Program, Boston University, *Honoring and Exploring the Sabbath.* He is the recipient of an Honorary Doctor of Divinity Degree from Morris College, Sumter, South Carolina and proudly serves on the Board of Trustees at that institution. In 2011, Dr. Carter was inducted into the Martin Luther King Board of Preachers, Morehouse College, in Atlanta, Georgia.

Dr. Carter loves to travel internationally and continues to take at least two international trips a year. He has extended his ministry to Haiti and has devoted time and resources to helping to rebuild that country and its people.

A great joy or Dr. Carter is going where he has never been before and getting the opportunity to experience other cultures, other languages and other types of people.

He is married to Cora and they are the parents of four adult children and the proud grandparents to Jabarite, Chad and Bradley.